Old Times – New Methods

Gábor Bertók – Csilla Gáti

ARCHAEOLINGUA

Budapest – Pécs

2014

Old Times – New Methods

Non-Invasive Archaeology in Baranya County (Hungary)
2005–2013

Gábor Bertók – Csilla Gáti

With support of the Culture 2007–2013 Programme of the European Union
(CU7-MULT7 Agreement Number 2010-1486 001-001)

This project has been funded with support from the European Commission.
This publication reflects the views only of the authors, and the Commission cannot be held responsible
for any use which may be made of the information contained therein.

The publication of this volume was funded by a generous grant from the National Cultural Fund (Nemzeti Kulturális Alap)

Front cover images:
Main image (continued on back cover): aerial photo of the Szemely 2 Late Neolithic enclosure
Right side strip: selected thumbnail pictures from the volume
Vertical strips: selected details from pictures from the volume

Back cover image:
(continued from front cover) aerial photograph of the Szemely 2 Late Neolithic enclosure (Gábor Bertók, 05. 08. 2006)

ISBN 978-963-9911-53-6

The following figures were created by Gábor Bertók using state copyrighted basemaps with permission of Dr. Bálint Papp,
(permission no. FF/1751/1/2013): I.8 b-c-d, I.47, I.49, II.2, II.5, II.9, II.15, II.20, II.26, II.30, II.36, II.39, II.42, II.53, II.56, II.66, II.70,
II.76, II.81, III.4, III.7, III.10, III.13, III.17, III.21, III.23, III.28, III.35, IV.17, V.3, VII.2, VIII.6, VIII.7, VIII.8, VIII.9, VIII.10, VIII. 11

The figures and maps presented in this volume are copyright of the authors named in the captions. Figures I.8, II.13, II. 56, II.63,
II.64, II.79, II.86, II.89, III.3, III.16 a-b, V.1, V.3, VI.1, VI.2, VII.1, VII.3, VIII.6-7-8-9-10, and VIII.11 were created by Gábor Bertók.

Figures IV.2, IV.3, IV.4, IV.10, IV.17, and the interpretive images attached to the aerial photographs were made by Csilla Gáti.

The magnetometer and ground penetrating radar surveys presented in this volume were made by Ecthelion Bt with
the exception of the magnetometer survey of the Szemely–Hegyes 1 enclosure complex which was surveyed by students
of Eötvös Loránd University, Dept. of Geophysics led by Mihály Pethe.

English translation: Gábor Bertók
Advice on this English edition was provided by Kevin Barton, Landscape & Geophysical Services

2014

Archaeolingua Alapítvány
1014 Budapest, Úri u. 49
www.archaeolingua.hu
Managing editor: Erzsébet Jerem

Copy editors: Emese Sarkadi Nagy, Ágnes Anna Sebestyén and Adrienn Zsiga-Hornyik
Desktop editing and layout: Gergely Hős
Cover design: Gergely Hős
Printing: AduPrint Printing and Publishing Ltd.

CONTENTS

I. Introduction

The present volume provides a snapshot of the most important results achieved during our non-destructive archaeological research campaigns carried out in Baranya County, Southwest Hungary, since 2005. The core material published here is based on the exhibition "Old Times, New Methods" we organized in 2012. Our research efforts have continued and we have had the opportunity to apply some "newer" methods that have further enhanced our understanding of the archaeological heritage of our county. Even though our work is still in progress, it has been worthwhile to publish an improved selection of the results representative of the eight years of non-destructive archaeological survey work we have carried out.

Between 2004 and 2007, the Department of Archaeology of the Janus Pannonius Museum participated in the European Landscapes – Past, Present and Future Project[1] funded by the EU Culture 2000 programme. The Project was carried out by 18 institutions from 15 countries. It was aimed at professionals, government agencies as well as the general public to demonstrate the effectiveness of non-destructive archaeological methods. The Project showed how these methods could be used in promoting the conservation of the archaeological elements of our common cultural heritage for future generations. For the first time in Baranya County, within the framework of the Culture 2000 Project, the Janus Pannonius Museum began a comprehensive aerial survey and field archaeological survey combined with a GIS-aided mapping project.

Following the successful conclusion of the European Landscapes – Past, Present, and Future Project in 2007, it was possible to continue survey work, albeit on a smaller scale, with the support of the National Cultural Fund of Hungary.[2]

I.1: The airplanes used for aerial archaeological reconnaissance by JPM (photo: G. Cs. – M. Kostyrko)

---

1   EU reg. no.: 2004-1495001-001-CLT CA22 European Landscapes – Past, Present and Future.
2   Project regs. nos NKA 6031/0010, 2731/0009, and 2731/105 2731/137.

I.2: Clearly discernible traces of a prehistoric earthwork near the town of Bóly. As indicated by surface finds, the structure could have been in use during several archaeological periods. (B. G. 02.09.2010)

I.3: The pits and other features of the settlement within the earthwork near Bóly showed up under different conditions compared to those in Fig. I.2. In this case, the conditions were mostly unfavourable for the appearance of the ditches. (B. G. 05.07.2011)

The invitation to participate as the only Hungarian co-organizer in the successful application for the ArchaeoLandscapes Europe Project (ArcLand, http://www.archaeolandscapes.eu) gave new impetus to our non-invasive survey and mapping activities. Supported by the European Commission's Culture 2007 framework programme, the ArcLand Project can be regarded as a continuation of the previous project, but on a much larger, pan-European scale. ArcLand involves 40 co-organizers and numerous associated partners from 27 countries. Extending beyond the previous project, ArcLand does not only include more participants, but places emphasis on the application of the latest non-invasive technologies such as airborne laser scanning, digital infrared photography and the integrated use of the various methods. Besides the improvement of research, it is equally important for the Project to create an international, self-sustaining network of professionals and to disseminate its achievements both for the professionals and the general public.

I.4: Cemetery of unknown date (possibly Roman or Avar) on the outskirts of the village of Pellérd (G. Cs. – B. G. 20. 06. 2013)

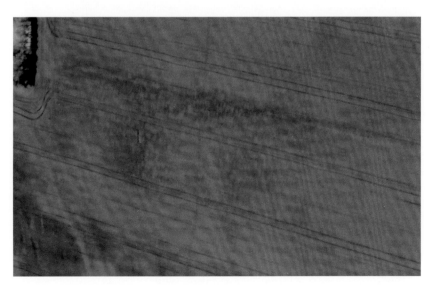

I.5: Infrared photograph of the Pellérd cemetery (G. Cs. – B. G. 20. 06. 2013)

I.6: The aerial archaeological sites photographed in Baranya County

I.7: Distribution map of the registered archaeological sites in Baranya (white) and the sites that have been photographed (red)

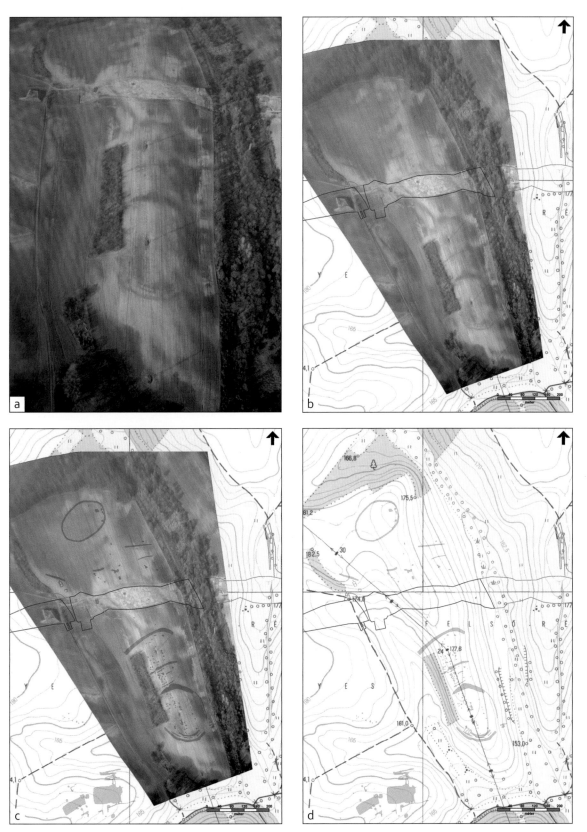

I.8: The workflow of photo interpretation and mapping: a) original oblique aerial photograph, b) digitally rectified aerial photograph overlaid on a topographic map, c) interpretation of suspected archaeological features, d) composite site map to aid further research and heritage management

About our aerial archaeological archive

Having become a basic method of site discovery and documentation in some European countries as early as the 1920s, aerial archaeological reconnaissance has since produced large collections of hundreds of thousands, or even millions of photographs. Though Hungarian aerial archaeological research had produced noteworthy results since its beginnings in the 1920s, the systematic application of aerial archaeological methods has only slowly gained ground since the early 1990s.

I.9: Using a Global Positioning System in the field   *I.10: Field-walking to recover surface finds*

When compared in numbers to the vast aerial archaeological archives, for instance, in the United Kingdom or Germany, even the earliest collections of Hungarian aerial archaeological archives at the University of Pécs, at the Hungarian Academy of Sciences and at the Eötvös Loránd University of Budapest are small, with each Hungarian archive adding up to some tens of thousands of photographs at most. However, they are all the more valuable considering the restricted resources and the short period of time that has elapsed since the start of their collection.

As a result of the previously mentioned grants from the European Commission, a new archive was established in 2005 at the Department of Archaeology of the Janus Pannonius Museum in Pécs. Presently, this collection contains more than 10,000 digital photographs showing potential archaeological sites and features, most of which are located in the central and south-eastern part of Baranya County.

The two grants from the EU have provided the necessary means to carry out systematic aerial reconnaissance campaigns of 6–10 flights per year, as well as the scanning of freely available satellite imagery. This has resulted in the discovery of more than 250 sites, including several earthworks, and soil- and cropmark sites of various archaeological periods that have been mapped, documented, and analyzed in a geographic information system.

Data collection

In recent years the examination of satellite imagery has quickly progressed as a means of site identification and mapping. This improvement has been made possible by some commercial companies that made a large number of high resolution images freely available through the Internet. These photographs are similar to regular aerial photographs in many respects as they allow the swift scanning of large areas. At the

I.11: Magnetometer survey in progress

same time, the available satellite images are already georeferenced, and thus they are suitable for basic interpretation and mapping. Additionally, images of the same area taken under various circumstances are usually also available, thus providing a diachronic view. In our research we have also used the above described means and up to the present we have discovered more than 20 archaeological sites from space.

More recently, we have obtained a high-resolution, handheld digital camera converted for near infrared photography. This camera shows the part of the invisible spectrum of light that vegetation reflects most intensively, thus providing details of archaeological features not always discernible in the visible light spectrum.

Taking aerial photographs, however, is only the first phase of our work; mapping and interpretation is equally important. Since the photographs are taken using a handheld camera, most of the time they are not taken with the camera pointed directly towards the ground beneath the aircraft. This results in a strongly varying scale and ground resolution within each oblique image. They also have other inherent distortions caused by the lens and the terrain. As a result, they are not immediately suitable for measurements and mapping. The first step in mapping is done through the photogrammetric correction of the oblique photographs. Provided that the input data, such as the focal length of the lens, the size of the sensor, the location and orientation of the camera at the moment when the picture was taken, etc., are known accurately, and a terrain model of suitable quality is available, photogrammetric correction of the image can be carried out. In this process sub-metre accuracy and a few centimetres/pixels ground resolution are achievable even when using a commercially available DSLR camera.

When loaded into a geographic information system, images transformed using the above methodology serve as a suitable base for mapping archaeological features that, in turn, can help and advance archaeological research.

However, the interpretation of aerial photographs and the mapping of features is only the first step in our work. To enhance the aerial archaeological information we have also analyzed archive data and carried out field-walking, geophysical surveys and trial trenching.

To survey large archaeological sites located in open, rural areas we have used magnetometry, a method most suitable for the detection and mapping of subtle magnetic anomalies caused by backfilled pits and ditches, subsurface remains of kilns, walls and other archaeological features. The disadvantage of magnetometry is that it cannot be used in areas where igneous rocks,

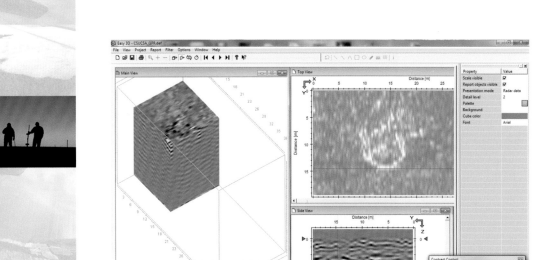

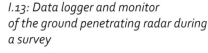

I.13: Data logger and monitor of the ground penetrating radar during a survey

I.12: Screenshot of ground penetrating radar processing: different views of an apse of a building at the Roman villa site at Bakonya–Csucsa-dűlő (see Chapter V). The stronger GPR reflections clearly indicate the well-preserved wall sections.

electric-powered machines, cables, industrial contamination, or other human activity cause strong magnetic anomalies. However, to survey magnetically undisturbed archaeological sites in open areas magnetometry is the quickest and the most effective method. As a result, we have surveyed several sites with a magnetometer including an Iron Age settlement, several Neolithic enclosures and a late medieval battlefield. The total area presently surveyed in Baranya County is 51 hectares.

In our work, we have also used ground penetrating radar, an effective tool to survey sub-surface remains of walls. As opposed to the magnetometer, this instrument can be used effectively in urban areas and even inside buildings containing, e.g., electric cables, metal fittings, and pipes. Though the interpretation of GPR images is often more difficult than magnetograms due to the many unknown factors that may cause or influence the reflections, we have some interesting results which are presented in this volume.

With the help of the ArchaeoLandscapes Europe project, we have had the opportunity to use another new remote sensing method; we have had 140 square kilometres surveyed using airborne laser scanning (ALS/LiDAR). The principle behind LiDAR is as follows: a high frequency laser scanner mounted on an aircraft equipped with a positioning system of very high accuracy, transmits laser beams and measures the reflections from the terrain below the aircraft. The timing, the direction, and the strength of the reflected signals are recorded by the instrument. Combined with the position of the aircraft at the moment of the individual laser emissions, the reflection data can be used to create a three dimensional point cloud that is processed to create a digital surface model. This model includes reflections from the terrain as well as from other objects, such as plants, buildings, electric cables, etc. By filtering, unnecessary data can be removed from the dataset, thus creating a terrain model. The terrain model may contain elements that represent traces of destroyed archaeological features, such as backfilled trenches and ploughed-out earthworks. The density of points depends on the frequency of the laser signal and the height and speed of the aircraft.

The nominal resolution of our filtered survey data is 8 points per square metre that is suitable for the detection of a number of archaeological features such as field boundaries, roads, plough marks, etc., even though the height differences within them are not more than a couple of decimetres at most.

The two most important results we achieved by applying the above described methods are that we quickly and cost-effectively gained detailed information on sites of large extent. In addition, we discovered formerly unknown relationships between individual sites and between the sites and the surrounding landscape. Perhaps the most significant among these discoveries was the fundamental change in our view of the Late Neolithic settlement system in our county through the discovery of numerous remains of Neolithic earthworks, and our observations concerning a possible network of Early Bronze Age fortified settlements. However, we must emphasize that this volume presents only a selection of highlights, and therefore does not contain all the sites in our collection. The entire material is available for research purposes at the Janus Pannonius Museum, Pécs.

We have carried out some of our work in collaboration with other institutions, among which the most important has been our joint investigations at the 1526 Mohács battlefield with the Institute and Museum of Military History of the Hungarian Ministry of Defense carried out since 2009. Some of our surveys were carried out during our training school in 2013 (NATS – *Non-Invasive Archaeological Training School*) with the help of the students and teachers.

The aerial photographs presented in this volume were taken by Gábor Bertók (B. G.), Csilla Gáti (G. Cs.), Béla Simon (S. B.), and Máté Szabó (Sz. M.). The majority of the photographs showing archaeological finds were taken by Anikó Tímárné Sinkó (T. S. A.) and István Füzi (F. I.). The vertical archive images are reproduced courtesy of the Institute and Museum of Military History of the Hungarian Ministry of Defense; the satellite images were saved from Google Earth.

II. Circles in the crop
Neolithic enclosed sites

Using the methods described in the Introduction, during our aerial and field surveys in Baranya County,[1] we have documented 33 partially destroyed earthworks belonging to various periods of the prehistoric era. Based on surface finds, 18 of these monuments certainly belong to the Late Neolithic Lengyel culture while another three or four may be considered Neolithic.[2] We expect to discover more of these earthworks during the course of further surveys.

Though the Neolithic settlement system in our area had not been surveyed in the field in a systematic way, results of earlier research, as well as the findings of large-scale rescue excavations in Western and Southern Transdanubia since 2000 have indicated a dense network of settlements, some of them including circular earthworks.[3] However, a breakthrough could only be achieved when systematic aerial and field surveys began in Baranya County in 2005.

Cropmarks in wheat near Pécs, Baranya County, revealing the remains of an enormous earthwork with an adjacent smaller, triple-ditched enclosure were photographed by Otto Braasch in 2003. He gave the photos of the enclosure he later nicknamed "Mother of all Henges" to the Aerial Archaeological Archive of Pécs, but the site was not examined any further at that time.[4]

Unaware of Braasch's results, we also "discovered" the site in 2005, right at the beginning of our first aerial survey campaign funded by the European Landscapes – Past, Present, and Future project. Surface finds indicated that the Szemely site, as well as a number of other circular earthworks photographed since belong to the same period, namely to the Late Neolithic Lengyel culture. These results gave impetus our efforts to investigate in detail the Late Neolithic settlements in our area.

Our work has taken place over 8 years and even now new sites still show up both during aerial surveys and on newly published satellite images. Our most recent discovery was a Neolithic enclosure in autumn 2012 at the site of Belvárdgyula–Gombás.

Our investigations have revealed a settlement system of much higher density and complexity than had been previously expected. It now appears that during the Late Neolithic, the construction of circular earthworks in association with large settlements is not a rare phenomenon in our area, but the natural way of using the landscape.

---

[1] The results of our investigations up to the end of 2006 at the Szemely–Hegyes site can be found in BERTÓK – GÁTI – VAJDA 2008; The geophysical survey map of the Belvárdgyula–Szarkahegy rondel was published in BERTÓK – GÁTI – LÓKI 2008 and 2009; BERTÓK – GÁTI 2009; BERTÓK – GÁTI 2011.

[2] The reason for the uncertainty comes from the fact that the latter enclosures "look like" the Neolithic ones, but we have not had the chance yet to collect dating material from them.

[3] See the inventory of South Transdanubian Lengyel sites in ZALAI-GAÁL 1982; KALICZ 1983–1984 for the rondels at Sé and Becsehely; ZALAI-GAÁL 1990a, 1990b about Mórágy, Kaposújlak–Várdomb-dűlő (SOMOGYI 2007), Sormás–Török-földek (BARNA 2005), Szólád–Kisaszó (OSZTÁS – MARTON – SÓFALVI 2004) és Nagykanizsa–Palin (TOKAI 2008).

[4] BRAASCH 2007, 89, 94; his unpublished photos of the Szemely site can be found in the Aerial Archaeological Archive of Pécs.

The case of the Belvárdgyula site provides a typical example where the settlement was found during field-walking that preceded motorway construction.[5] The site was partially uncovered in 2007 and 2008 as part of rescue excavations, and a rondel was discovered during aerial reconnaissance on the northern edge of the settlement in 2007. The following year we carried out a magnetometer survey and surface find collection that proved the settlement and the rondel to be contemporary.

Proved by the results of subsequent geophysical survey, the discovery of the rondel at the well-known Lengyel site of Zengővárkony in 2007 was unexpected. Large areas of the settlement had already been excavated in the 1930s and 1950s by J. Dombay. He uncovered more than 350 graves and numerous settlement features. Dombay did not find any traces of major earthworks even though he was among the first archaeologists experimenting from an aerial perspective: he had the site and its surroundings surveyed and photographed from the air in 1939.[6] Ironically, the comparison of his maps with our rectified aerial photographs and geophysical survey map shows that by accident he dug his trenches all around the rondel, never touching it. Therefore, he had no chance to become aware of the complexity of the structure of the Zengővárkony settlement, no matter how thorough his efforts were. The latest results show, that – no matter what we could achieve using a different approach – our knowledge of the site is still incomplete. Published by Google in 2012, a satellite image shows an oval enclosure 260 m in diameter in the field next to the southeast edge of what was considered as "the Zengővárkony Lengyel site". Surface finds indicate that this feature also belongs to the Lengyel period. Though not a typical Lengyel rondel, this oval enclosure has good parallels in our area and may rather be considered as one that enclosed either an entire settlement or a part of it.

Having also been investigated in the 1950s by J. Dombay, another formerly known Lengyel site lies near the village of Villánykövesd. Dombay field-walked and trial-trenched the Late Neolithic settlement and found it to extend over an area larger than a square kilometre.[7]

His excavation results were similar to those at Zengővárkony: he identified groups of graves and "dwelling pits", but could not gather more information on the general layout of the site.

István Zalai-Gaál performed the first aerial archaeological survey of the Villánykövesd area in 1987. Being a researcher of the Late Neolithic, he specifically looked for rondels and other settlement features of the period, and he took pictures of the Villánykövesd site where he identified several soilmarks as possible rondels. He published his findings in 1990, but no further efforts were made to investigate the implication of his findings[8].

During our aerial and field surveys we also identified and photographed the site, noting that at least one circular enclosure lay next to the settlement, while the surface finds proved its Late Neolithic date. Between 2009 and 2011, we had the opportunity to survey the suspected rondel with a magnetometer. Always showing up in aerial photographs as a poorly defined, double circular mark, the enclosure turned out to be a highly complex structure of two major concentric ditches with several regular interruptions, augmented by U-shaped extensions on its outer perimeter. Within the main ditches ran palisades, of which the outer one had a triple row.

---

5   BERTÓK – GÁTI – LÓKI 2008.
6   DOMBAY 1939, 1960; LENGVÁRI 2009.
7   DOMBAY 1959. 58.
8   ZALAI-GAÁL 1990a, 1990b.

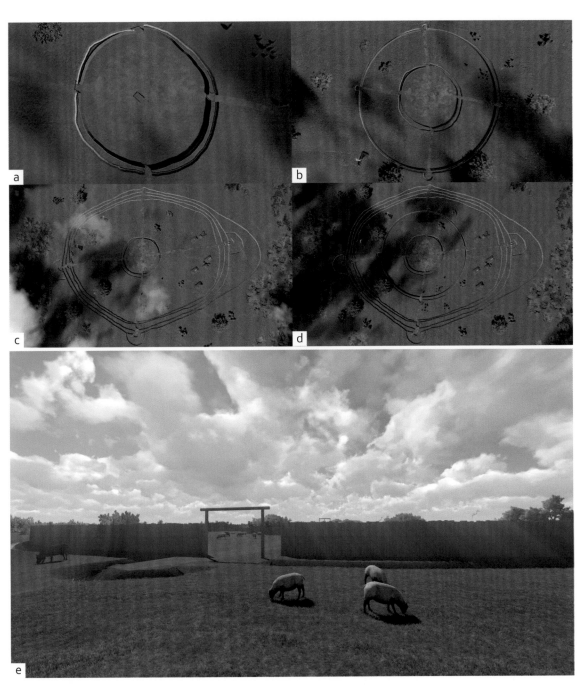

II.1: Hypothetical reconstruction of various suspected phases of the Szemely I enclosure complex (a, b, c), and a general 3D reconstruction of all the ditches and palisades detected through magnetometry and excavation (d). Below (e): a reconstructed view from the Szemely I enclosure towards the Szársomlyó Hill, 3D graphics by Csaba Pozsárkó

Regarding the U-shaped ditch extensions, we know analogies from only a few South Transdanubian sites: Szólád,[9] Nagykanizsa[10] and Kaposújlak[11] in Somogy County, and Szemely in Baranya County.

The interior of the structure seems sparsely utilized apart from its northern side where 2 or 3 longhouses and other traces of habitation can be found. The houses may be contemporary, as they seem to be in alignment with the inner palisade.

Several of the Late Neolithic earthworks found in Baranya County seem to fit into the "classical" category of rondels/*Kreisgrabenanlagen*. As such, these earthworks may be characterized by a cultic/communal function, but they exceed most of their parallels in Austria, Slovakia and Germany[12] both in size and complexity.

However, there is another type of earthworks we have identified in our area of research. The builders of these enclosures did not intend to create structures of a regular circular plan; the surface finds suggest that these earthworks of irregular oval plan surrounded entire settlements and possibly served a defensive purpose, such as those at Magyarsarlós, Feked, Nagykozár, and maybe the outer ditches of the larger enclosure at Szemely.

Accordingly, from the viewpoint of settlement structure in the region there were:

- open settlements without any (known) earthworks (such as Pécsvárad–Aranyhegy, Borjád–Kenderföldek);
- large open settlements without surrounding defensive structures, but with circular enclosures associated with them (Villánykövesd–Jakabfalusi út mente, Belvárdgyula–Szarkahegy, Máriakéménd–Szellői-sarok, Töttös–Alsó megye-dűlő, Vokány–Falu végi rész, Szebény–Farkaslik-dűlő, Kökény–Temetői-dűlő, Harkány–Szilágy);
- large settlements (4–7 ha) entirely surrounded by earthworks of possible defensive purpose (Magyarsarlós–Kerekes-dűlő, Nagykozár–Zámájur-dűlő, Feked–Lapos, Palkonya–Gréci-dűlő, and possibly Belvárdgyula–Gombás);
- settlements including both types of earthworks (Szemely–Hegyes, Belvárdgyula–Nádas, Zengővárkony–Igaz-dűlő, Geresdlak–Hosszú-hát, Peterd–Gyomberek).

This varied settlement typology is, of course, a temporary one since the data sources used to create the plans are not uniform. However, this diversity may still be the first direct evidence of an otherwise logical supposition: the 600–700 year long period of the Late Neolithic in our area was not uneventful; it had its own history of peaceful and violent phases to which the population tried to adapt. At the same time, these earthworks serve as proof of the economic power of the communities that were capable of providing for their members taking part in their construction and maintenance.

---

9   Osztás – Marton – Sófalvi 2004, Pl. XX. 3.
10   Tokai 2008.
11   Somogyi 2007, 343.
12   For summaries on the subject see: Trnka 1991, Petrasch 1990, Kovárník 2003, Kuzma 2005, Melichar – Neubauer 2010.

Therefore, we can conclude that presently we have a far more detailed picture of the Late Neolithic earthworks and settlement structure than before the start of our integrated survey. We not only know of more of these features, but we have also gained significant knowledge of their internal structure, and can distinguish several types of enclosure and types of settlement. However, it is a task for further research to reveal whether these differences have a chronological, functional, social or other significance.

From a methodological point of view, we can draw the conclusion that the integrated use of various remote sensing and other non-invasive methods in archaeological prospecting can fundamentally change our knowledge of the archaeological heritage of an area.

In the following chapter, we present a complete catalogue and a typological table of all the known Late Neolithic sites of relevance discovered in Baranya County.

Catalogue

1. Belvárdgyula–Gombás

Location: south of the village Belvárdgyula, on a plateau overlooking the valley of a west-east running stream
Outer diameter: 180–190 m
Number of ditches: 2
Width of ditches: ca. 2 m
Enclosed area: 3 ha (estimated)
Entrances: 2 gateways are visible on the southwest and north side, both having a U-shaped ditch

Description: surrounded by several features showing up as soilmarks, a partially discernable enclosure of two narrow, concentric ditches shows up on Google Earth satellite imagery, and as a cropmark in wheat in subsequent aerial photography. Field-walking of the site produced Neolithic pottery.
Sources: Google Earth, field-walking, aerial photography
Date: Neolithic

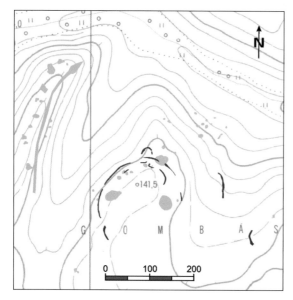

II.2: Map of the soil and cropmark features at the Belvárdgyula–Gombás site

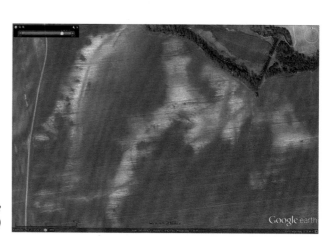

II.3: Satellite image of the Belvárdgyula–Gombás site (08. 03. 2012)

II.4: Aerial photoraph of the Belvárdgyula–Gombás site (B. G. – G. Cs. 20. 06. 2013)

2. Belvárdgyula–Nádas

Belvárdgyula–Nádas 1

Location: between the villages of Belvárdgyula and Szederkény, on a long, flat plateau enclosed by the valleys of two streams that meet at its southern end
Outer diameter: 550×300 m on the outside; inner rondel: 120 m
Enclosed area: ca. 13–14 ha (estimation based on transcribed aerial photographs)
Number of ditches: 4 in 2 groups in the outer enclosure, 2 in the internal rondel
Width of ditches: 2–5 m (based on transcribed aerial photographs)
Entrances: cannot be identified as yet

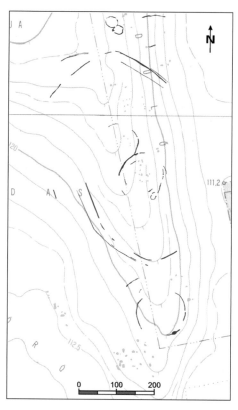

Belvárdgyula–Nádas 2

Location: 60–70 m south of Belvárdgyula–Nádas 1
Outer diameter: 130 m
Enclosed area: 1.2 ha
Number of ditches: 1
Width of ditch: 1–1.5 m
Entrances: cannot be discerned

II.5: Map of the aerial archaeological features at the Belvárdgyula–Nádas site

Description: Located in the field called Nádas, partially discernible traces of a composite enclosure were spotted from the air in 2010. The site shows similarities to that at Szemely–Hegyes in its complexity. Two double ditches surround an area of 550×300 m in size; in the centre lies a presumably double ditched rondel. Though only vaguely discernible, there is another possible enclosure adjacent to the northwestern edge of the rondel. There are numerous pits and other features in and around the Nádas 1 enclosure complex, 70 m to the south of which lies the single ditched (palisaded?) Nádas 2 enclosure.

The single, extensive field-walking survey we have had the opportunity to carry out so far produced Late Neolithic pottery, but, of course, we do not have detailed information on the distribution of finds and on the chronology of the highly complex, 2 km long site. When compared with Zalai Gaál's description, the Belvárdgyula–Nádas site can be identified with site No. 5 in his 1982 paper listing the then known South Transdanubian Lengyel sites. In our aerial photographs taken in June 2013, two smaller ring-ditches show up near the northern edge of the Nádas 1 enclosure. According to our present knowledge, these ring-ditches are uncharacteristic of the Lengyel culture, and may indicate that the site was in use in other archaeological periods, too.
Sources: literature, aerial photographs, satellite imagery, field-walking
Date: Late Neolithic (Lengyel culture)
Literature: Zalai-Gaál 1982, 5

II.6: Satellite image of the Belvárdgyula–Nádas site (08. 03. 2012)

II.7: Aerial photograph of the Belvárdgyula–Nádas site (B. G. – G. Cs. 20. 06. 2013)

II.8: Aerial photograph of the Belvárdgyula–Nádas site (B. G. – G. Cs. 20. 06. 2013)

3. Belvárdgyula–Szarkahegy

Location: on a plateau northwest of Belvárdgyula, 300 m north of the M60 Motorway
Outer diameter: 215×200 m
Area including the ditches: 3.3 ha
Enclosed area: 1.54 ha
Number of ditches: 2 and a palisade ditch
Entrances: 3 are known from the magnetic survey, a 4th is likely to be on the south side

Description: In 2006 and 2007, a rescue excavation was carried out on the route of the M60 Motorway on the outskirts of the village of Belvárdgyula. It was already obvious then that the motorway would cut a Late Neolithic settlement and cemetery.

Excavation and field-walking data showed that the motorway excavation covered the southern edge of the site, and the bulk of the settlement lay to the north.

During an aerial photography sortie aimed at documenting the progression of excavations along the motorway route, we noticed a circular enclosure on the northern perimeter of the settlement. In 2008, further field-walking and a geophysical survey were carried out to acquire dating information and a detailed plan of the site. The results showed that the enclosure was contemporary with the adjacent settlement. The geophysical survey also indicated that the rondel enclosure had had elaborate gate structures that were destroyed and levelled most probably in the Neolithic, and therefore the details of their structure cannot be discerned in the magnetogram. There are several features showing up as magnetic anomalies. Based on their shape and size, some of these anomalies may be identified as houses. This was the first site in our county where the close relation between a settlement and a rondel could be demonstrated.

Sources: rescue excavation, aerial photography, geophysical survey
Date: Late Neolithic (Lengyel culture)
Literature: BERTÓK – GÁTI – LÓKI 2008, 2010; BERTÓK – GÁTI 2011

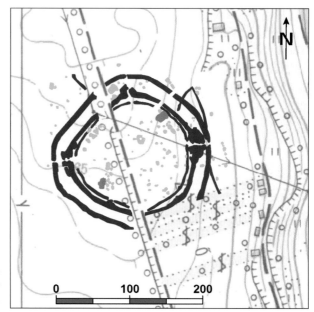

II.9: Map of the Belvárdgyula–Szarkahegy Late Neolithic enclosure based on the geophysical survey results

*II.10: Satellite image
of the Belvárdgyula–Szarkahegy site*

*II.11: Belvárdgyula–Szarkahegy, aerial photograph
of the rondel that shows its location relative
to the motorway excavation site (B. G. 31. 05. 2007)*

29

← *II.12: A close-up photo of the rondel in wheat crop (B. G. 31. 05. 2007)*

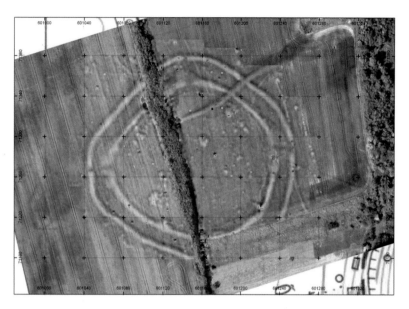

II.13: Belvárdgyula–Szarkahegy, the magnetogram overlaid on the rectified aerial photograph

II.14: Finds from the rescue excavation of the Belvárdgyula–Szarkahegy Late Neolithic settlement (excavation of Olivér Gábor, photo: T. S. A.)

4. Feked–Lapos

Location: north of the road between the villages of Feked and Erdősmecske, on a plateau slightly rising to the north
Outer diameter: 206×240 m
Number of ditches: 2 narrow (palisade?) ditches
Width of ditches: ca. 2 m (based on aerial photography)
Enclosed area: 5 ha
Entrances: 2 are discernible, 1 on the northern and 1 on the western side

Description: Presumably surrounded by a double palisade, the slightly hexagonal, rounded enclosure has cropmarks inside and around that may be indicative of a settlement. Including several pieces of pottery and an obsidian blade, the majority of the surface finds belong to the Late Neolithic period, although some Roman finds were also recovered.
Sources: Aerial photographs, satellite imagery, field-walking.
Date: Late Neolithic (Lengyel culture)

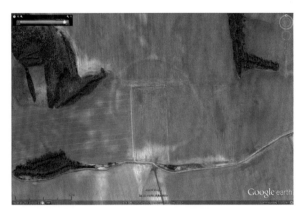

II.16: Feked–Lapos in satellite imagery (18. 03. 2010)

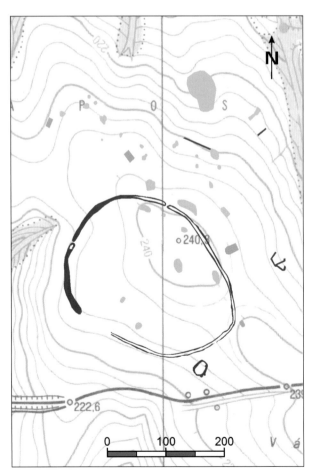

II.15: Map of the Feked–Lapos Late Neolithic enclosure based on rectified aerial photographs

*II.17: Aerial photograph of the Feked–Lapos
enclosure under various crops (B. G. 16. 07. 2007)*

II.19: The Feked–Lapos enclosure showing up as a soilmark (B. G. 02. 10. 2008)

← *II.18: The Feked–Lapos enclosure: partial soil/cropmark (B. G. – G. Cs. 31. 08. 2011)*

5. Geresdlak–Hosszú-hát

Geresdlak–Hosszú-hát 1

Location: south of the village of Geresdlak, on the northwestern end of a north-south elongated plateau
Outer diameter (of the rondel): 150 m
Enclosed area: 1.8 ha
Number of ditches: 2 visible, a possible 3rd is faintly discernible on the outside
Width of ditches: 3–5 m (based on aerial photography)
Entrances: cannot be discerned, but there is a possible interruption on the western side of the rondel in the suspected third, outermost ditch that surrounds both the rondel and the settlement

Geresdlak–Hosszú-hát 2

Location: south of the village of Geresdlak, on the southern end of a north-south elongated plateau
Outer diameter: 180–200 m
Enclosed area: 2.9 ha
Internal area: 0.91 ha
Number of ditches: 1
Width of ditch: 3–5 m (based on aerial photography)
Palisades: there are 3 concentric traces 1–2 m in width running inside the main enclosure
Entrances: 1 to the west and 1 to the south are visible

Description: *Enclosure complex 1* can only partially be discerned in aerial photography. Being remains of a settlement, a great number of pits are visible as soilmarks north of rondel enclosure no. 1. A linear soilmark seems to surround both the rondel and the settlement features. Its visible section is ca. 420 m long. North of the double ditched rondel, the faint traces of another possible enclosure are visible.
Rondel 2 is located near the southern tip of the elongated hill, 1 km south of Enclosure complex 1. The rondel has a regular, round plan comprising ditches and palisade(s) showing up as soilmarks. The northwestern quarter of the outermost ditch runs into a steep gully. There are several hundred pits in and around *Rondel 2*.
The relationship of the two enclosure complexes and the features between them is uncertain at the moment.
Sources: aerial photographs and satellite imagery, field-walking
Date: Late Neolithic (Lengyel culture)

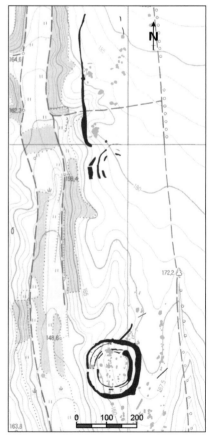

Il.20: Map of the Geresdlak–Hosszú-hát enclosures, based on aerial photography

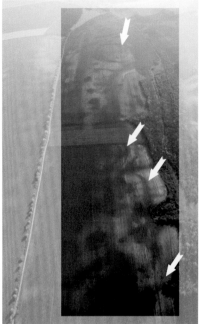

*Il.21: Geresdlak–Hosszú-hát,
aerial photograph showing the two
enclosure-complexes from the north
(no. 1 in the foreground, no. 2
in the background; B. G. 18. 11. 2008)*

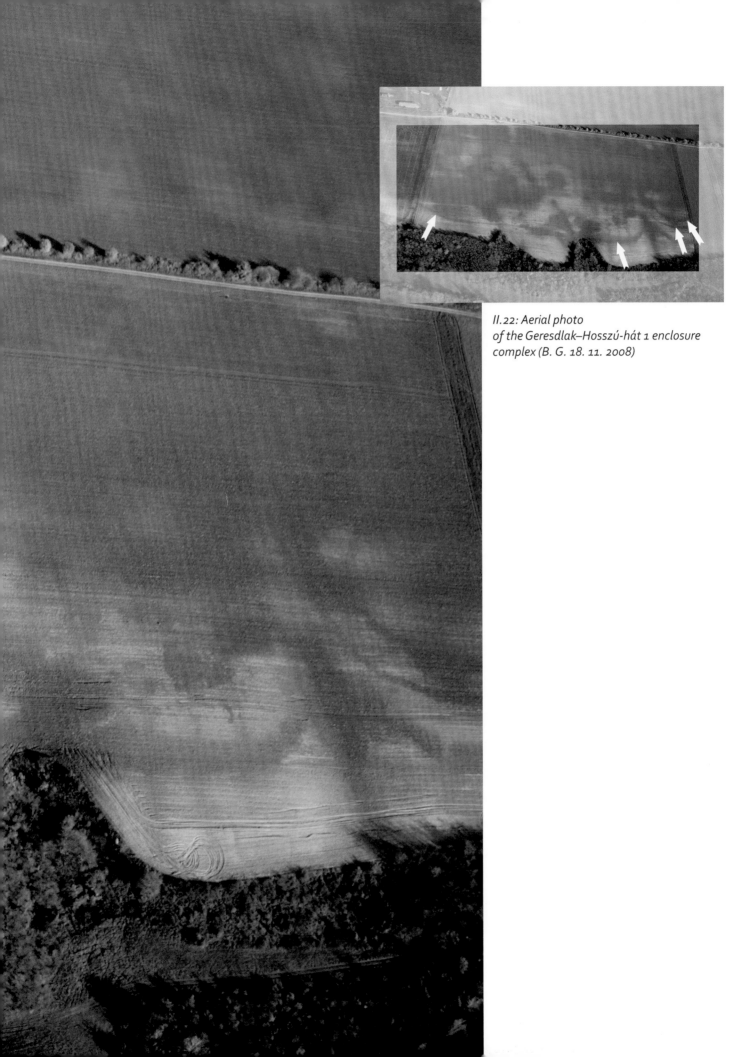

*II.22: Aerial photo
of the Geresdlak–Hosszú-hát 1 enclosure
complex (B. G. 18. 11. 2008)*

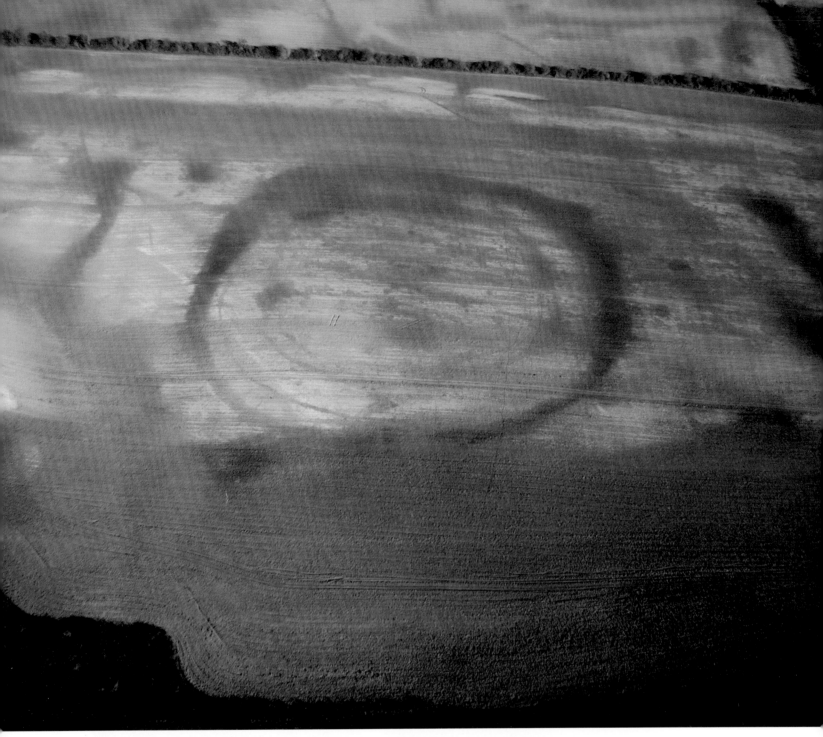

II.25: Aerial photograph of the Geresdlak–Hosszú-hát 2 enclosure (B. G. 18. 11. 2008)

↖ *II.23: Aerial photograph of the Geresdlak–Hosszú-hát 2 enclosure (B. G. – G. Cs. 06. 06. 2012)*

← *II.24: Aerial photograph of the Geresdlak–Hosszú-hát 1 enclosure complex (B. G. 18. 11. 2008)*

6. Harkány–Szilágy

Location: on a gently sloping area 1 km north of Harkány, on the edge of the one-time flood-plain of the Drava River
Outer diameter: 290 m
Entire area: 6.1 ha
Enclosed area: ca. 0.8 ha
Entrances: not discernible
Number of ditches: 3
Width of ditches (cropmarks): 10–15 m

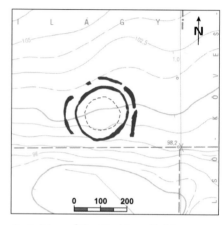

Description: Partially visible rondel-like, triple-ditched enclosure with no other archaeological features showing up around it. In and around the enclosure there are numerous finds dated to the Middle Bronze Age. However, there are Neolithic finds too, though they are not characteristically Late Neolithic. Therefore, the dating of the enclosure is as yet uncertain.
Sources: aerial and satellite imagery, field-walking
Date: Neolithic/Bronze Age(?)

II.26: Map of the Harkány–Szilágy enclosure based on satellite images and aerial photographs

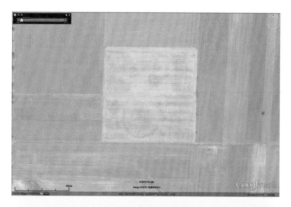
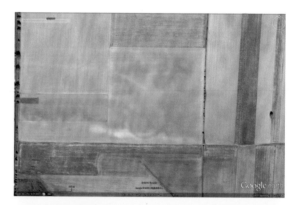

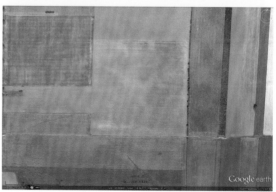

II.27: The Harkány–Szilágy enclosure in satellite imagery under various land-use conditions

II.28: Aerial photograph of the Harkány–Szilágy enclosure (B. G. 29. 06. 2005)

II.29: Aerial photograph of the Harkány–Szilágy enclosure (B. G. 18. 04. 2006)

7. Kökény–Temetői-dűlő

Location: to the east-southeast of the village of Kökény, on a promontory extension of a plateau bordered by a sinuous, steep slope on the north

Outer diameter: ca. 200 m

Entire area: 3.1 ha

Enclosed area: 1.8 ha

Number of ditches: 3, and traces of a 4th, palisade ditch inside the three main ditches

Entrances: not discernible in aerial photographs, geophysical surveys indicated an entrance to the north

Description: We have field-walked the site twice, but we have not found any surface finds except for 2 pieces of medieval pottery. There is a Late Copper Age (Baden–Pécel culture) settlement 200 m northeast of the rondel, and Late Neolithic, Lengyel culture finds were reported from the area east of the village.

Sources: aerial photographs and satellite imagery, field-walking, geophysical survey

Date: unknown, circumstantial evidence suggest Late Neolithic or Late Copper Age

Literature: BÁNDI – PETRES – MARÁZ 1979, 41, Site no. 17; ZALAI-GAÁL 1982, 5, Site no. 17, with further literature

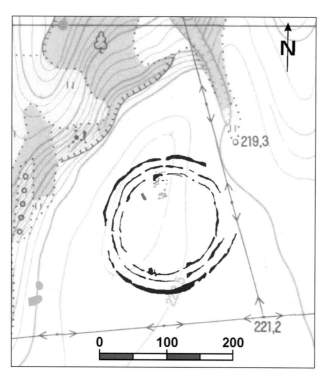

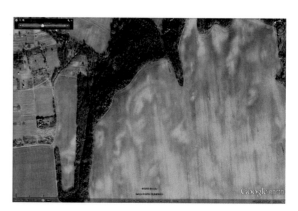

II.31: Satellite image showing the Kökény–Temetői-dűlő rondel (05. 02. 2007)

II.30: Plan of the Kökény–Temetői-dűlő rondel enclosure based on orthorectified aerial photographs and magnetometry

II.33: Aerial photograph
of the Kökény–Temetői-dűlő rape crop in full
bloom (B. G. – G. Cs. 07. 05. 2011)

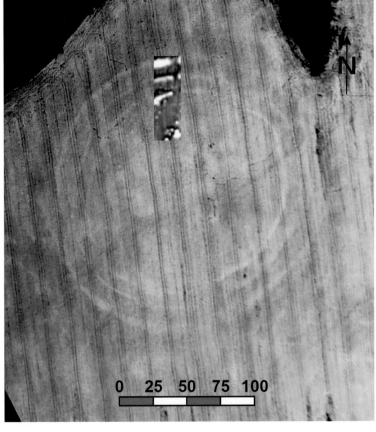

*II.34: Aerial photograph
of the Kökény–Temetői-dűlő in rape crop
at the end of blooming
(B. G. – G. Cs. 14. 06. 2011)*

0 25 50 75 100

*II.35: Kökény–Temetői-dűlő:
magnetogram overlaid
on the orthorectified aerial
photograph of the rondel
(surveyed during NATS 2013 Pécs)*

8. Magyarsarlós–Kerekes-dűlő

Location: near the edge of the plateau immediately to the north of the village of Magyarsarlós
Outer diameter: 360×260 m
Enclosed area: larger than 6 ha; the exact area cannot be determined due to the eroded southern part of the enclosure
Number of ditches: 1
Width of ditch: 6–8 m (soilmark)
Entrances: not visible in the aerial photographs and satellite images

Description: The enclosure is likely to be a fortified settlement: the enclosure is oval not showing the characteristics of a typical rondel. Finds of mostly flint nodules and flakes with a few pieces of Lengyel pottery were found within the ditch.
Sources: aerial photographs and satellite imagery, field-walking
Date: Late Neolithic (Lengyel culture)

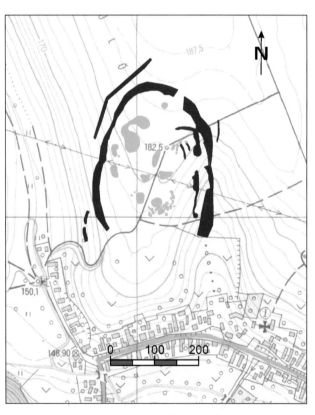

II.36: Plan of the Magyarsarlós–Kerekes-dűlő enclosure based on an orthorectified aerial photograph

II.37: Satellite image showing the Magyarsarlós–Kerekes-dűlő enclosure (05. 02. 2007)

II.38: Aerial photograph showing the Magyarsarlós–Kerekes-dűlő enclosure (B. G. 09. 12. 2008)

9. Máriakéménd–Szellői-sarok

Location: northeast of the village of Máriakéménd, on the western part of a wide plateau surrounded on three sides (west, south, east) by stream valleys
Outer diameter: 130 m
Enclosed area: ca. 0.59 ha
Number of ditches: 1
Width of ditch: the soilmark indicating the enclosure is 15–20 m wide; the true width of the ditch is likely to be much narrower
Entrances: 1 possible entrance facing southwest is visible in the images

Description: Our field-walking did not produce finds from the area of the single-ditched enclosure, but 70 m south of it we found Middle Neolithic (Linearbandkeramik?) pottery sherds in a small area. In the aerial photographs, soilmarks indicating pits and a linear feature could be identified 150 m to the south of the enclosure, where we found Celtic pottery. Therefore, the dating of the enclosure is dubious.
Sources: aerial photographs and satellite imagery, field-walking
Date: possibly Middle Neolithic

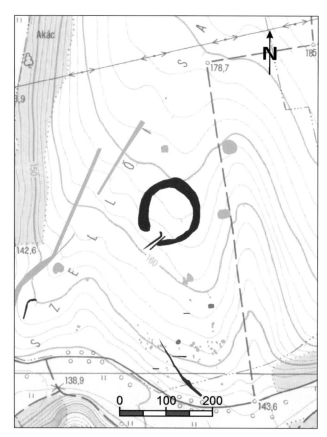

II.40: Satellite image showing
the Máriakéménd–Szellői-sarok rondel

II.39: Map of the Máriakéménd–Szellői-sarok rondel

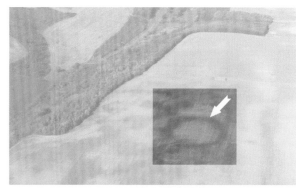

II.41: Aerial photograph of the Máriakéménd–Szellői-sarok site (B. G. 04. 10. 2006)

10. Nagykozár–Zámájur-dűlő

Location: southwest of the village of Nagykozár, on a plateau surrounded on three sides by stream valleys
Outer diameter: 330×230 m
Entire area: 5.5 ha
Area of inner enclosure: 1 ha
Number of ditches: 2 ditches are well defined, and there is a possible 3rd one
Width of ditches: 5–8 m (soilmarks)
Entrances: could not be securely identified

Description: An enclosure compound consisting of at least two oval ditches with a possible annex enclosed by a third ditch. The majority of the finds recovered during field-walking were chipped stone flakes and a few pottery sherds. Some pottery shards dated to the Lengyel culture had been recovered during an earlier field-walking from the site.
Sources: aerial photographs and satellite imagery, field-walking
Date: Late Neolithic (Lengyel culture)
Literature: BÁNDI – PETRES – MARÁZ 1979, 41, Site no. 23

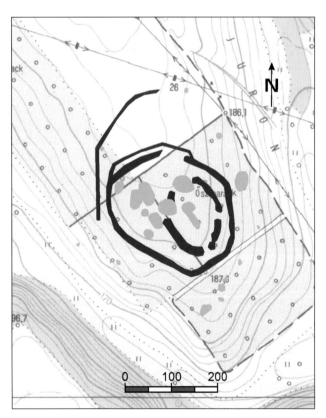

II.43: Satellite image of the Nagykozár–Zámájur-dűlő enclosure (05. 02. 2007)

II.42: Map of the Nagykozár–Zámájur-dűlő enclosure based on aerial and satellite images

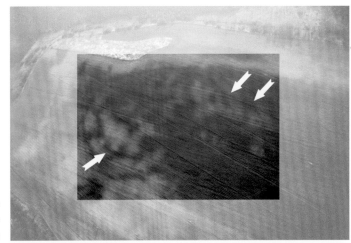

*II.44: Aerial photograph
of the Nagykozár–Zámájur-dűlő enclosure
(B. G. 13. 02. 2008)*

II.45: Digital infrared photograph of the Nagykozár–Zámájur-dűlő enclosure (B. G. 07. 01. 2012)

II.46: Aerial photograph of the enclosure near Nagykozár (B. G. 18. 04. 2006) →

11. Palkonya–Gréci-dűlő

Location: west of the village of Palkonya on a wide plateau surrounded on three sides by stream valleys
Outer diameter: at least 280×200 m (estimated)
Entire area: at least 4 ha
Number of ditches: possibly 2
Entrances: cannot be determined

Description: A settlement site surrounded by at least 2 ditches. Very few Late Neolithic finds were recovered from the area of the enclosure; one of these was a ceramic sherd from a thin-walled vessel with a knob typical of Lengyel pottery.
Sources: aerial photographs, field-walking
Date: probably Late Neolithic (Lengyel culture)

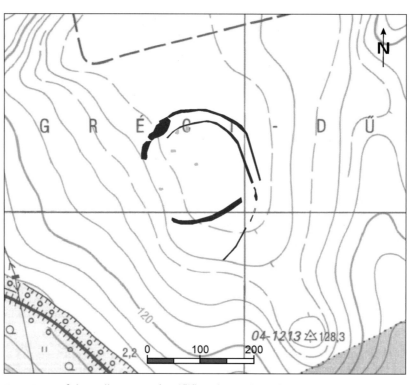

II.47: Map of the Palkonya–Gréci-dűlő enclosure based on aerial photographs

II.48: Aerial photograph showing the Palkonya–Gréci-dűlő enclosure (B. G. – G. Cs. 25. 04. 2013)

12. Peterd–Gyomberek

Location: southwest of the village of Peterd on a plateau surrounded on three sides by stream valleys
Outer diameter: ca. 400×250 m
Diameter/area of rondel: 110 m/0.95 ha
Number of ditches: at least 1 in the outer enclosure; 2 forming the rondel (one of which may be a palisade)
Width of ditch (measurable at the rondel): 2–3 m
Palisade: the inner ditch of the rondel may be that of a palisade
Entrances: discernible on the east side

Description: An enclosure complex consisting of a rondel inside a slightly hexagonal (or possibly pentagonal) enclosure whose southern border is not seen in the available imagery. Resembling the nearby Szemely 1 enclosure complex, there is a trace of a path entering the inner area across the eastern gates. Our field-walking produced Late Neolithic and few medieval pottery shards.
Sources: aerial photographs and satellite images, field-walking
Date: Late Neolithic (Lengyel culture)

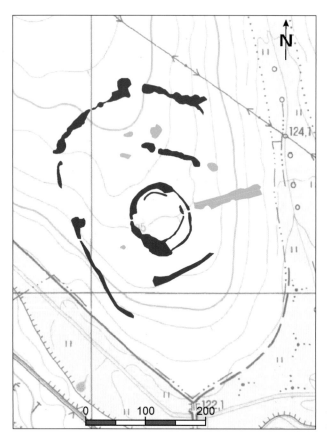

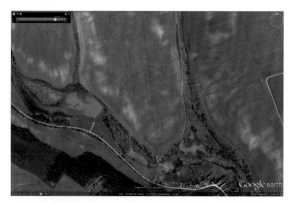

II.50: Satellite image of the Peterd–Gyomberek enclosure complex (18. 03. 2012)

II.49: Map of the Peterd–Gyomberek enclosure complex based on an aerial photograph

II.51: Aerial photograph showing the Peterd–Gyomberek enclosure complex (Aerial Archaeological Archive of Pécs Inv. no. 44880, courtesy of M. Szabó 30. 06. 2012)

II.52: Aerial photograph showing the Peterd–Gyomberek enclosure complex (B. G. – G. Cs. 31. 05. 2012)

59

13. Szebény–Farkaslik-dűlő

Location: southeast of the village of Szebény, on an elongated hill bordered on the west and the east by two stream valleys. The rondel is surrounded by several large, pit-like soilmarks

Outer diameter: 110–120 m

Entire area: ca. 1 ha

Enclosed area: 0.44 ha

Number of ditches: 2

Width of ditches (soilmarks): 3–5 m

Entrances: 1 is faintly visible on the east

Description: J. Dombay excavated graves dated to the Lengyel period in the field called Farkaslik-dűlő in 1939, but finds belonging to another archaeological period (Middle Bronze Age) have also been mentioned as originating from here. Based on its size, shape, and arrangement, the rondel-like double-ditched enclosure showing up in our aerial photographs and in a satellite image (Bing Maps) is likely to belong to the Lengyel period.

Sources: excavation, aerial photographs and satellite imagery

Date: possibly Late Neolithic (Lengyel culture)

Literature: BÁNDI – PETRES – MARÁZ 1979, 42; Site no. 34; 93, Site no. 40

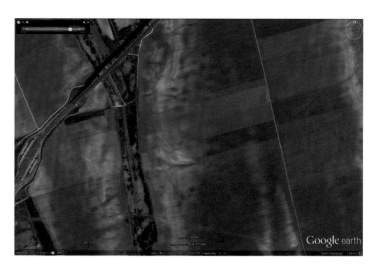

II.54: Satellite image of the Szebény–Farkaslik-dűlő rondel (10. 03. 2012)

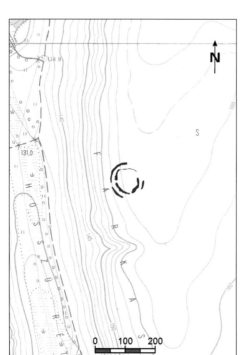

II.53: Plan of the Szebény–Farkaslik-dűlő rondel enclosure based on a satellite image

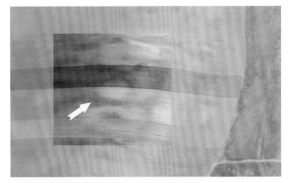

II.55: Aerial photograph of the Szebény–Farkaslik-dűlő rondel (18. 11. 2006)

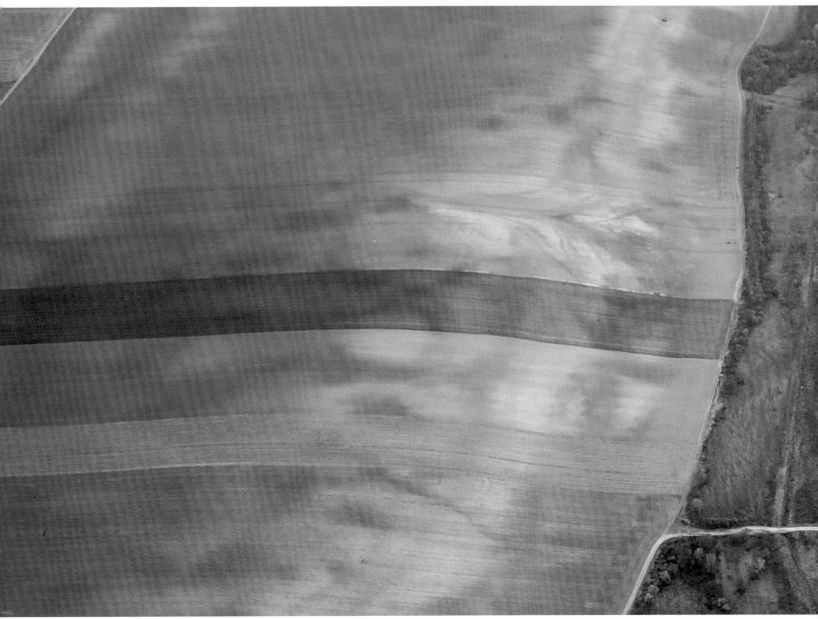

14. Szemely–Hegyes (Szemely–Bregova)

Szemely–Hegyes 1

Location: northeast of the village of Szemely on a long, hill bordered by the valleys of two confluent streams
Outer diameter: 530×390 m
Entire area: 8.4 ha with an additional annex of 1.1 ha at the south
Diameter of/area enclosed by the middle enclosure: 200 m/3.6 ha
Diameter of/area enclosed by the innermost rondel: 100 m/0.5 ha
Number of ditches:
- outer enclosure complex: forming a rounded hexagon, 4 concentric, ca. 2 m wide, ca. 2 m deep, V-shaped ditches surround the entire enclosure complex; enclosing an annex 1.1 ha in size, the outermost ditch diverges from the others around the south gate;
- middle enclosure: a single, V-shaped ditch, ca 2–3 m deep, most probably intentionally backfilled and levelled ditch;
- innermost rondel: and a single, but re-cut, 2.5–3.5 m deep ditch with V-shaped section.
Palisades: 1 partially rebuilt palisade within the innermost rondel enclosure; 1 on the outside of the entire complex (visible only around the northern half of the structure)
Entrances: There are 4 gates approximately facing the cardinal directions with the axis defined by the north and south gates having a 17 degrees declination to the west and east, respectively. Apart from the inner rondel, there are U-shaped ditch extensions of various sizes around each gate, except the eastern gates where they are missing. However, in the east there is a path forming a depression that shows up both in the LiDAR and magnetic data. The path runs through the eastern gates and enters the area between the middle enclosure and the inner rondel where it disappears. A similar path can be observed at the Peterd–Gyomberek site (Cat. no. 12).

Szemely–Hegyes 2

Location: 200 m to the south of Szemely–Hegyes 1 on the same hill
Outer diameter: 170×155 m including, 155×142 m excluding the ditch extensions before the gates
Entire area: 1.73 ha
Enclosed area: 0.43 ha
Number of ditches: 3, with the innermost and the middle ditch having been re-cut
Width of ditches: 3–4 m
Palisade: 1 within the innermost ditch, its width being 0.8–1 m
Entrances: there are 4 gates approximately facing the cardinal directions with the axis defined by the north and south gates having an 11 degrees declination to the west and east, respectively

Description: Extending to 9.5 hectares and having a diameter more than 0.5 km, the larger Szemely 1 enclosure complex consists of three concentric sets of ditches. The smaller Szemely 2 enclosure lies 200 m to the south of the Szemely 1 complex. It is only 1/5 in size when compared to the larger one. As it was expected, the trial trenches dug in 2006 at Szemely 1 produced material dating to the Late

Neolithic Lengyel culture: red painted ware, chipped and polished stone tools, an antler hoe, and large quantities burnt daub fragments. The ditches were V-shaped and 2–3 m deep.

Simultaneously with the excavation, students led by M. Pethe from the Eötvös Loránd University Department of Geophysics carried out a magnetic gradiometer survey that covered the larger part of the Szemely 1 enclosure complex. The survey results provided information on the layout of the enclosure without the need for further excavations. Among the most interesting details were the semicircular ditches placed around the outer side of the entrances.

In 2008, we continued our research by first surveying with magnetic gradiometry then trial-trenching the Szemely 2 enclosure. We dug the southwest-northeast running, 50 m long trial trench perpendicular to the three ditches.

As a result of the magnetic surveys and the excavations we improved the plan of both enclosure complexes: it turned out that the triple segmentation of both structures indeed exists. Reaching down at places to 3–4. 5 m, several of the ditches were re-cut. The magnetic surveys also revealed a great number of other features within and between the two enclosures. These findings will facilitate the planning of further research activities.

We have also discovered that there are semicircular ditch extensions attached to the outer ditch sections in groups of 2 and 3 between and around the gates at the Szemely 2 enclosure.

Unfortunately, the means and depth of research we have had the opportunity to achieve has not yet made the determination of the relative chronology of the two enclosure complexes possible. It may be possible that the picture provided by the aerial photographs and the magnetogram is a diachronic imprint that shows elements that may have evolved and decayed through several centuries and may have not existed contemporaneously.

Sources: JPM Archive, aerial photographs and satellite imagery, field-walking, excavation, C14 dating

Date: Late Neolithic (Lengyel culture) (based on two C14 samples, the Szemely 1 enclosure complex is likely to have existed at least between 4900 and 4600 BC)

Literature: PUSZTAI 1956, 39–44; BÁNDI – PETRES – MARÁZ 1979, 42, Site no. 38; ZALAI-GAÁL 1982, 6, Site no. 40; BERTÓK – GÁTI – VAJDA 2008; BERTÓK – GÁTI 2011

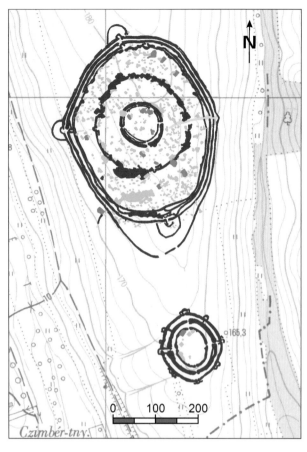

II.58: Aerial photograph
of the Szemely–Hegyes site as soilmarks
(B. G. 08. 04. 2006) →

II.56: Plan of the Szemely–Hegyes enclosures
based on magnetometer survey data

II.57: Aerial photograph of the Szemely–Hegyes
enclosures (B. G. 05. 08. 2006)

II.59: Aerial photograph of the Szemely–Hegyes 2 rondel enclosure (B. G. 05. 08. 2008)

II.60: Archive vertical aerial photograph of the area around Szemely–Hegyes. The enclosure complex Szemely 1 is revealed as a faint trace. (1978, HM-HIM Archive Inv. No. 47485)

II.61: The enclosures of the Szemely–Hegyes site showing up as snowmarks (B. G. – S. B. 29. 01. 2010)

II.62: Features at Szemely–Hegyes
in the excavations of 2006

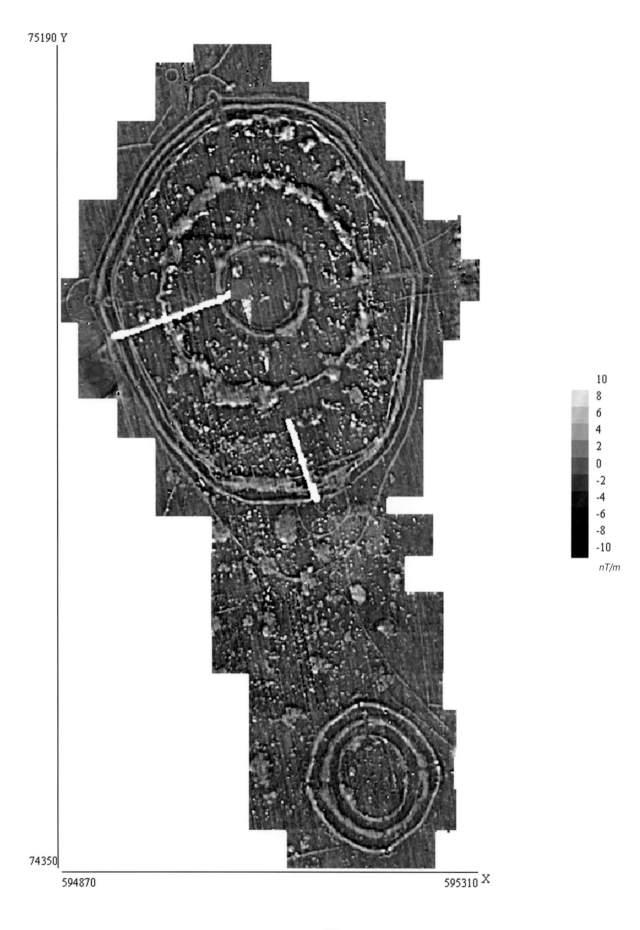

75190 Y

74350

594870   595310 X

10
8
6
4
2
0
-2
-4
-6
-8
-10
nT/m

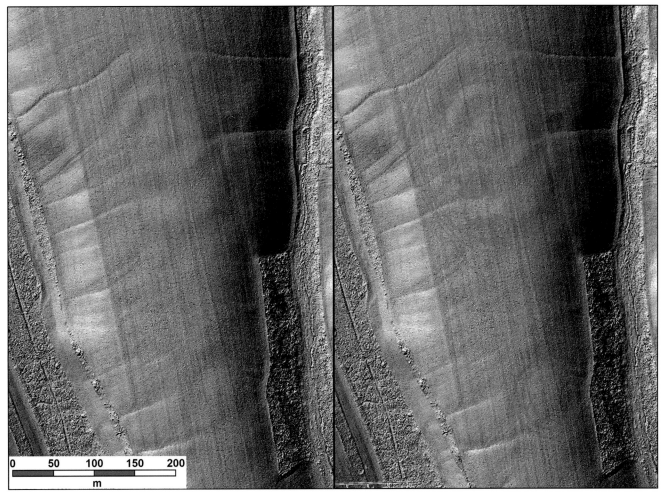

II.64: The plan of the two Szemely enclosures overlaid on a shaded relief map created from high-resolution LiDAR data. The course of the ditches is clearly visible as slight undulations in the terrain.

II.65: Finds from the excavation of the Szemely–Hegyes enclosure complex 1 (photo: T. S. A.)

← *II.63: Magnetogram of the Szemely–Hegyes enclosures*

69

15. Töttös–Alsó megye-dűlő

Location: southwest of the village of Töttös, on a plateau surrounded on three sides (southwest, southeast, northeast) by stream valleys
Outer diameter: 160 m
Entire area: 2 ha
Enclosed area: 1.18 ha
Number of ditches: 2
Palisade: could not be seen
Width of ditches: 2–3 m (cropmarks/soilmarks)
Entrances: have not been seen in the imagery so far

Description: Most possibly belonging to the group of Late Neolithic rondels, the double-ditched enclosure of regular, circular shape seems to have been surrounded by an open settlement, as indicated by the surface finds and features showing up in aerial photographs.
Sources: JPM Archive, aerial photographs, field-walking
Date: Late Neolithic (Lengyel culture)

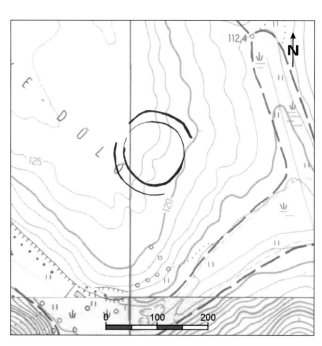

II.66: Outline of the Töttös–Alsó megye-dűlő rondel enclosure based on a rectified aerial photograph

II.67: Near infrared image of the Töttös–Alsó megye-dűlő site (B. G. – G. Cs. 10. 03. 2012)

II.68: The Töttös–Alsó megye-dűlő rondel as cropmarks in maize (B. G. – G. Cs. 31. 08. 2011)

II.69: The Töttös–Alsó megye-dűlő rondel as soilmarks, on the opposite hilltop traces of possible archaeological features can be seen (B. G. – G. Cs. 10.03.2012)

16. Villánykövesd–Jakabfalusi út mente (Villánykövesd–Bogdács)

Location: north of the village of Villánykövesd, in a wide, flat area west of the dirt track that leads to Jakabfalu
Outer diameter: 305×310 m (including the extensions that block the causeways)
Number of ditches: 2
Width of ditches: 3–5 m at the narrower parts of the magnetic anomalies showing the main ditches; the palisade ditches are 1.2–1.5 m in width
Palisades: a triple row between the main ditches and a single palisade inside the inner ditch (magnetic anomaly)
Enclosed area: 170×150 m, ca. 2.13 ha
Entrances: there are 13 causeways/interruptions visible on the outer ditch, all of them blocked on the outside by U-shaped ditches; the inner enclosure has 7 or possibly 8 causeways

Description: J. Dombay, the then director of the County Museum, directed a small-scale excavation near the village of Villánykövesd in 1957. His investigations showed that the site comprised a settlement with scattered groups of graves covering an area as large as a square kilometre. Based on the finds, Dombay dated the site to the period of the Late Neolithic Lengyel culture.

Apart from its extent, and the few graves and pits excavated in 1957, further details of the plan of the settlement remained unknown until 1987, when the archaeologist I. Zalai-Gaál flew a single sortie in the area searching for Neolithic sites. He discovered traces of a circular earthwork near Villánykövesd and identified it as a Neolithic rondel.

Since the beginning of our aerial archaeological campaign and field surveys in 2005, our repeated visits to the site have confirmed I. Zalai-Gaál's observations. The rondel-like enclosure some 300 m in diameter showed up several times, but only as a blurred, circular mark.

Based on orthorectified aerial photographs, we set up a grid to survey the rondel with a magnetometer. The survey was done in 2009 and 2011. The site plan arising from the survey results clearly shows why it is worth combining several methods of prospection: the enclosure was unknown until discovered from the air, but cropmarks and soilmarks only provided information on the size and general layout of the structure, but little detail. In turn, the magnetic survey that revealed much detail could not have been carried out effectively without the preliminary information gained from aerial photographs.

The Villánykövesd enclosure turned out to comprise several unique features when compared with other Late Neolithic rondels. Its outer ditch, 300 m in diameter, is interrupted at regular 50 m intervals and the interruptions are blocked by protruding, semi-circular extensions. The function of these extensions is unknown. They have some analogies; near the villages of Szemely, Kaposújlak, and Szólád as well as near the town of Nagykanizsa. The closest analogy to the type of interrupted ditch with semicircular extensions is that at Kaposújlak. Though similar in structure, the Kaposújlak ditch is not circular but linear and blocks the entrance to a hilltop whose shape resembles a promontory. This means that the usual cultic/astronomical interpretation associated with rondels is not plausible here. Because of its linearity and location, the structure at Kaposújlak may be indicative of the defensive nature of the semicircular extensions, an interpretation that may also apply at Villánykövesd.

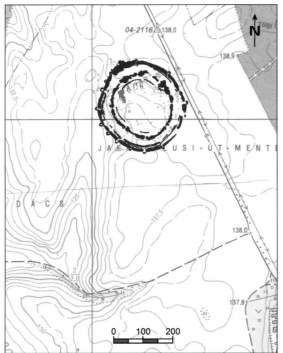

II.71: Satellite image showing the Villánykövesd enclosure

II.70: Plan of the Villánykövesd–Jakabfalusi út mente enclosure based on magnetometer survey data

II.72: Finds from the excavations led by J. Dombay at Villánykövesd

In the centre of the Villánykövesd enclosure, traces of 2 or 3 houses were found – an uncommon feature in Late Neolithic rondels. The inner palisade and the houses appear to be more or less contemporary since they are placed parallel to and not overlapping with each other, as if they were planned and built taking the other structure into consideration.

We could also identify anomalies that seem to indicate 2 or 3 longish houses. these buildings are likely to be contemporary with the enclosure since they were aligned to the inner palisade.

Sources: excavation by J. Dombay, aerial photographs, field-walking, geophysical survey

Date: Late Neolithic (Lengyel culture)

Literature: DOMBAY 1959; ZALAI-GAÁL 1990, 1990a; BERTÓK – GÁTI 2011

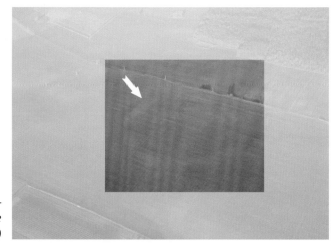

*II.73: Aerial photograph of the Villánykövesd–
Jakabfalusi út mente enclosure
(B. G. 06. 10. 2006)*

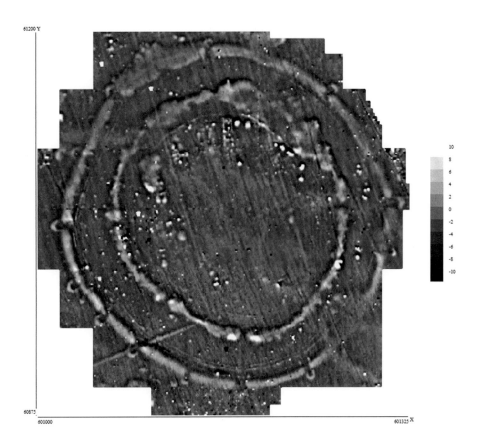

II.74: Magnetogram of the Villánykövesd–Jakabfalusi út mente enclosure

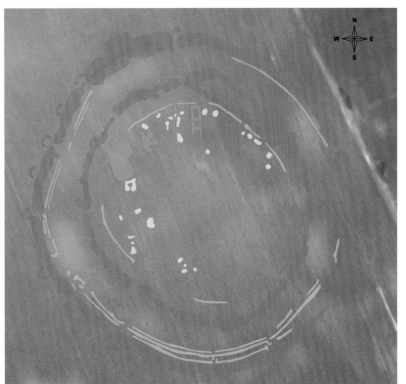

II.75: The magnetogram of Fig II.74 overlaid on the rectified aerial photograph

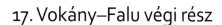

17. Vokány–Falu végi rész

Location: southeast of the village of Vokány, on a wide plateau surrounded on three sides (west, south, east) by stream valleys
Outer diameter: 210×200 m
Entire area: 3.25 ha
Enclosed area: 0.78 ha
Number of ditches: 4 (2 of them are possible palisades)
Width of ditches: 2–5 m (cropmarks)
Entrances: a possible eastern entrance is visible in aerial photography

Description: I. Zalai-Gaál discovered the multiple-ditched Vokány rondel enclosure from the air in 1987. Based on its plan, he dated the enclosure to the Late Neolithic Lengyel period. His photos showed a possibly double-ditched, circular soilmark feature of unclear outline, as it was also the case with us until 2010. Since then, the rondel appeared in a sugar beet crop (2010) and in a wheat crop (2013) showing much detail. It appears that within the two wide, outer ditches there are at least two narrower rows on the inside. These latter cropmarks may be indicative of palisades. The few finds we managed to recover from the area of the enclosure are mostly uncharacteristic, but seem to be Neolithic. It has to be mentioned though that 400 m from the rondel, on the same plateau, there are pits visible in aerial photographs where we found Bronze Age pottery sherds.
Sources: aerial photography, field-walking
Date: Late Neolithic (Lengyel culture)
Literature: ZALAI-GAÁL 1990, 1990a

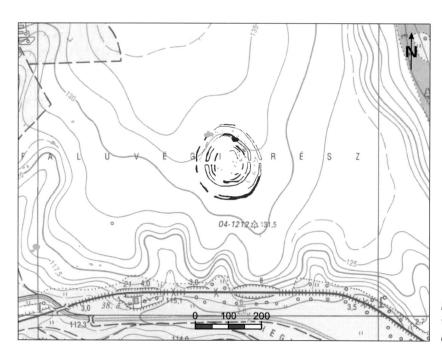

II.76: Plan of the Vokány–Falu végi rész rondel based on rectified aerial photographs

II.77: The Vokány rondel visible in a sugarbeet crop (B. G. – G. Cs. 02. 09. 2010)

II.78: Aerial photographs of the Vokány–Falu végi rész site as soilmarks (B. G. 18. 04. 2006)

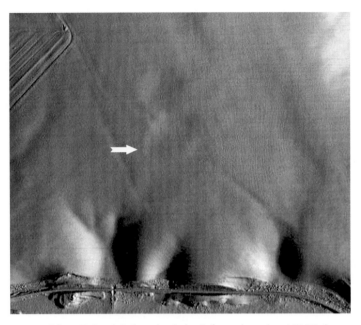

II.79: Vokány–Falu végi rész: shaded relief map based on LiDAR data

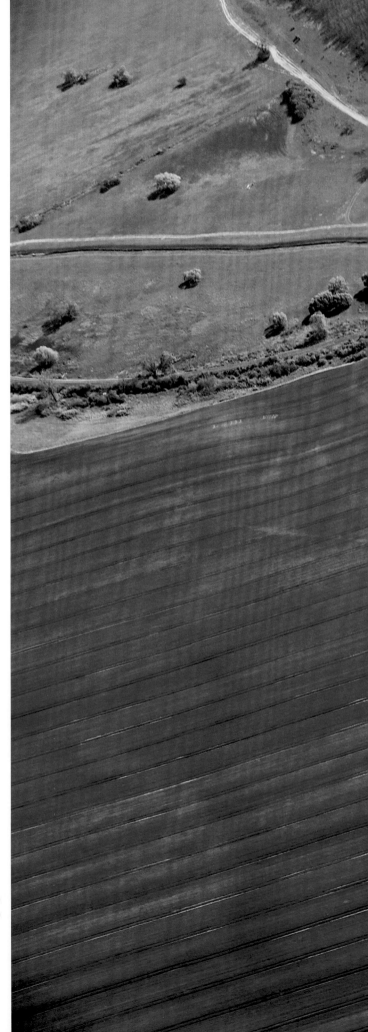

II.80: The Vokány rondel visible in a wheat crop
(B. G. – G. Cs. 15. 04. 2013)

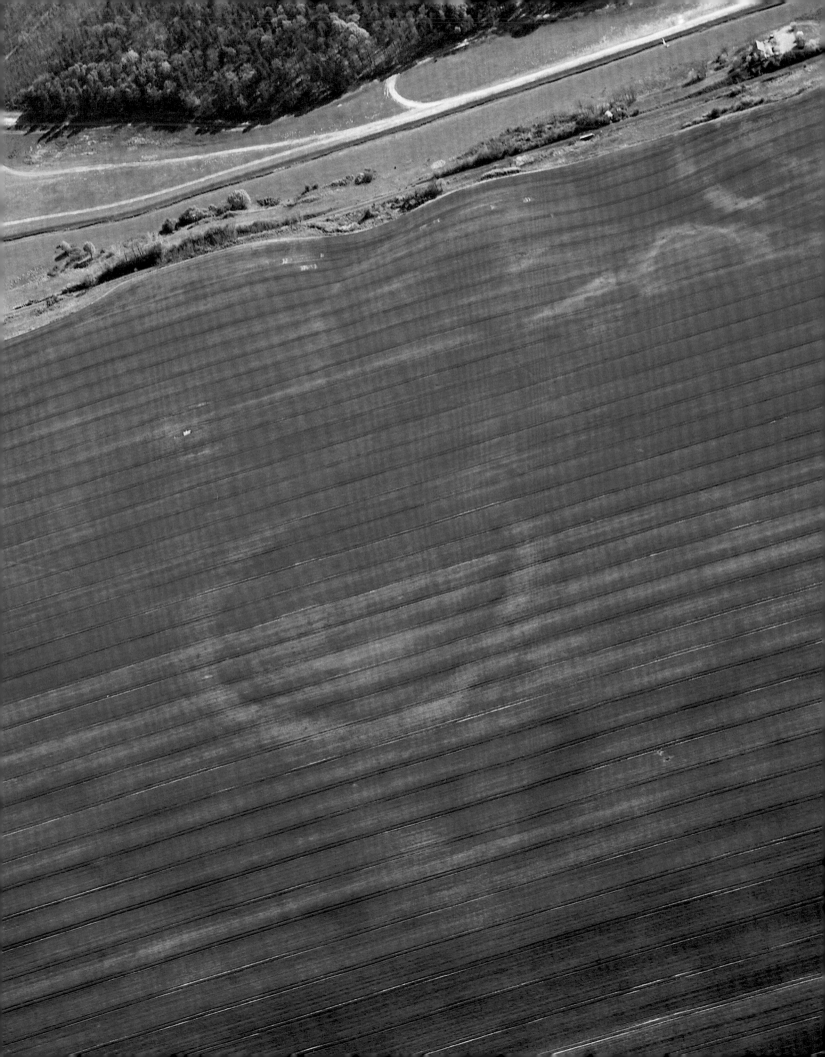

18. Zengővárkony–Igaz-dűlő

Zengővárkony–Igaz-dűlő 1

Location: north-northwest of the village of Zengővárkony, cut by the old Road 6, on a promontory, part of a wide plateau
Outer diameter: 180 m north-south × ca. 160 m west-east; because of the partially overlying road and shrubbery, the west-east diameter of the rondel can only be estimated
Entire area: ca. 2.2 ha
Enclosed area: ca. 0.9 ha
Number of ditches: 2, both seem to have been re-cut
Width of ditches: 2–5 m (magnetogram)
Entrances: 3 are visible (facing to the west, north, and south; a 4th, eastern gate can also be postulated)
Sources: excavations by J. Dombay, field-walking, aerial photographs and satellite images, magnetic gradiometer survey

Zengővárkony–Igaz-dűlő 2

Location: 430 m to the south-southeast of the Zengővárkony 1 enclosure, on a gentle slope facing southwest
Outer diameter: 250×180 m
Area: 3.9 ha
Number of ditches: 1 (possibly 2)
Entrances: cannot be seen
Sources: satellite image, field-walking

Description: The Late Neolithic settlement and cemetery have been known since the 1930s due to the investigations by János Dombay, the then director of the County Museum. He carried out excavations in the 1930s and 1940s and published his findings in German in two volumes. He excavated numerous settlement features, as well as several groups of burials. However, he only managed to excavate a small part of the site as it extends over 40 hectares.

János Dombay's publication of the finds was regarded as setting a standard, both in terms of quality and quantity, in research for a long period of time. He described a large number of finds of all kinds recovered from various contexts: pottery vessels, stone and bone tools, jewellery and ritual artefacts from nearly 400 graves and other features. However, his excavations produced little information on the layout of the settlement.

Having flown over the site in 2008, we discovered faintly discernible cropmark traces that indicated pits and an oval or circular enclosure (Zengővárkony 1). The subsequent geophysical survey proved that the cropmarks were those caused by various settlement features, including the backfilled double ditches of a rondel.

In 2012 we discovered the traces of another possible earthwork (Zengővárkony 2) to the south of the Zengővárkony 1 rondel. Our field-walking produced few Neolithic pottery shards and flint flakes. Since the enclosure is likely to belong to the formerly known Zengővárkony-Igaz-dűlő site, we list it here.

Date: Late Neolithic (Lengyel Culture)

Literature: DOMBAY 1939, 1959; ZOFFMANN 1972–73; BERTÓK – GÁTI 2011

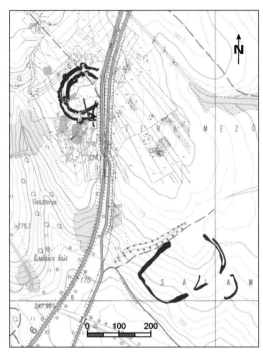

II.81: Map of the Zengővárkony 1 and 2 enclosures based on geophysical survey data, aerial photographs, and satellite images

II.82: Satellite image of the Zengővárkony–Igaz-dűlő 2 enclosure

II.83: Archive aerial photograph of the Zengővárkony site obtained by J. Dombay in 1939 (after LENGVÁRI 2009)

II.84: Aerial photograph of the Zengővárkony 1 rondel (B. G. 19. 06. 2008)

II.85: Infrared photograph of the Zengővárkony 1 rondel (10. 03. 2012) →

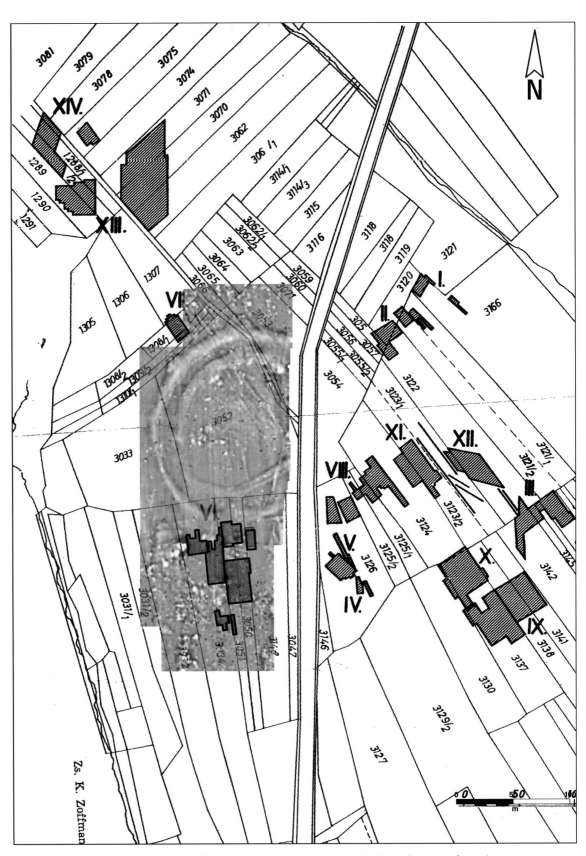

II.86: The magnetogram of the Zengővárkony 1 rondel enclosure overlaid on the map of Dombay's excavations (after ZOFFMANN 1972–73, Plan 1)

II.87: Aerial photograph of the Zengővárkony 1 rondel (B. G. 19. 06. 2008)

II.88: Aerial photograph of the Zengővárkony 1 rondel (B. G. 19. 11. 2009)

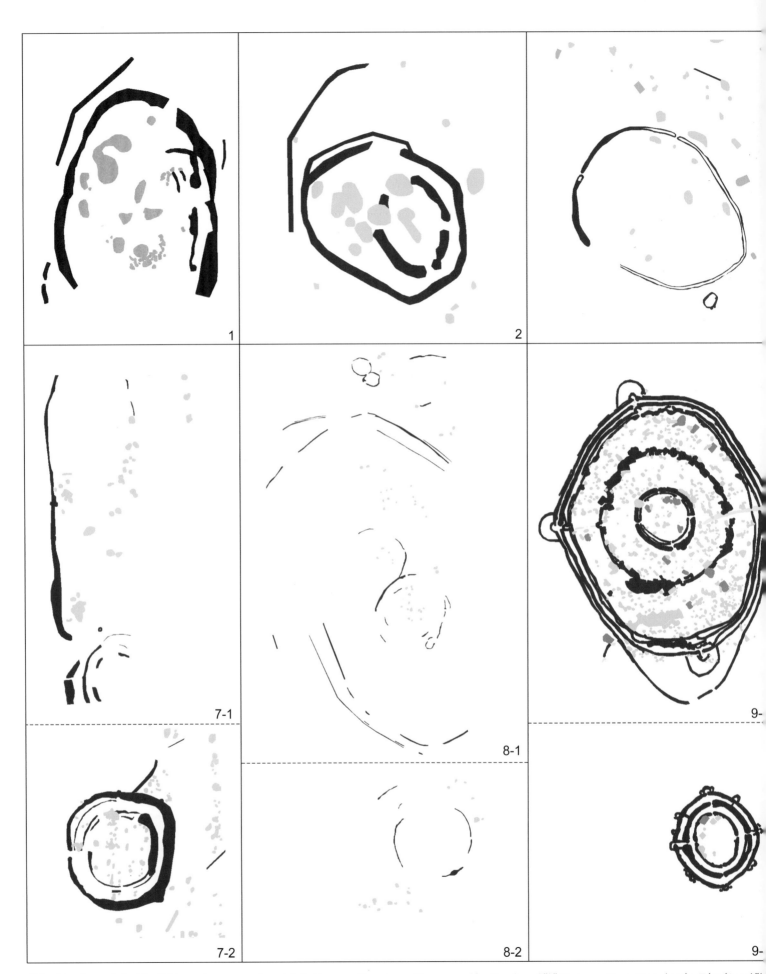

II.89: Typology of the Neolithic enclosures and rondels in Baranya County **1.** Magyarsarlós–Kerekes-dűlő (Cat. no. 8) **2.** Nagykozár–Zámájur–dűlő
6. Zengővárkony–Igaz-dűlő (Cat. no. 18) **7.** Geredlak–Hosszú-hát (Cat. no. 5) **8.** Belvárdgyula–Nádas (Cat. no. 2) **9.** Szemely–Hegyes (Cat. no. 14
Szellői-sarok (Cat. no. 9) **13.** Harkány–Szilágy (Cat. no. 6) **14.** Szebény–Farkaslik-dűlő (Cat. no. 13) **15.** Töttös–Alsó megye-dűlő (Cat. no. 15

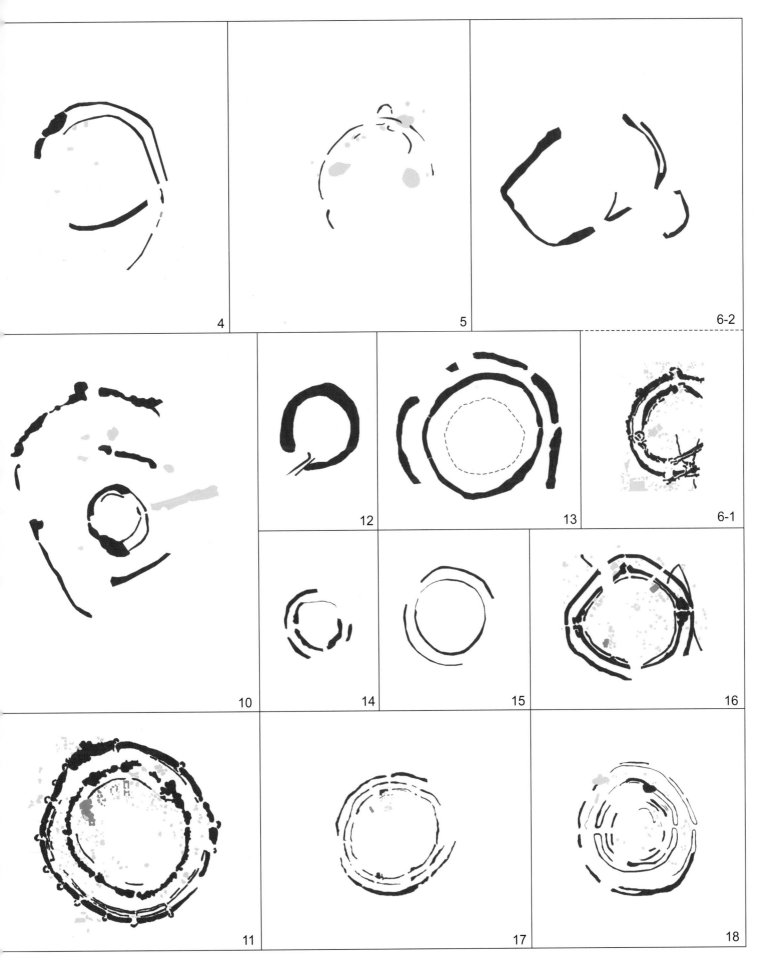

(Cat. no. 10) **3.** *Feked–Lapos (Cat. no. 4)* **4.** *Palkonya–Gréci-dűlő (Cat. no. 11)* **5.** *Belvárdgyula–Gombás (Cat. no. 1)*
10. *Peterd–Gyomberek (Cat. no. 12)* **11.** *Villánykövesd–Jakabfalusi út mente (Cat. no. 16)* **12.** *Máriakéménd–*
16. *Belvárdgyula–Szarkahegy (Cat. no. 3)* **17.** *Kökény–Temetői-dűlő (Cat. no.7)* **18.** *Vokány–Falu végi rész (Cat. no. 17)*

0   50   100   150   200   N

II.90: Distribution map of the Neolithic earthworks, numbered according to the Catalogue

90

Literature

BÁNDI – PETRES – MARÁZ 1979
BÁNDI, G. – PETRES, É. F. – MARÁZ, B.: Baranya megye az őskorban. A Lengyeli kultúra. In: Bándi G.: *Baranya megye története az őskortól a honfoglalásig*. Pécs 1979, 19–57.

BARNA 2005
BARNA, J. P.: Sormás–Török-földek településtörténeti áttekintése. A középső neolitikum (The history of a settlement at Sormás–Török-földek. Middle Neolithic). *Zalai Múzeum* 14 (2005) 17–37.

BERTÓK – GÁTI – VAJDA 2008
BERTÓK, G. – GÁTI, Cs. – VAJDA, O.: Előzetes jelentés a Szemely–Hegyes lelőhelyen (Baranya megye) található neolitikus körárok-rendszer kutatásáról (Preliminary report on the research at the neolithic Kreisgrabenanlage at Szemely–Hegyes, Baranya county, Hungary). *AÉ* 133 (2008) 85–106.

BERTÓK – GÁTI – LÓKI 2008
BERTÓK, G. – GÁTI, Cs. – LÓKI, R.: Előzetes jelentés a Belvárdgyula határában (Baranya megye) talált késő neolitikus település és körárok kutatásáról (Vorbericht über den Forschungstand der spätneolithischen Siedlung und Kreisgrabenanlage in der Gemarkung von Belvárdgyula, Komitat Baranya). *Ősrégészeti Levelek* 10 (2008) 5–17.

BERTÓK – GÁTI 2011
BERTÓK, G. – GÁTI, Cs.: Neue Angaben zur spätneolithischen Siedlungsstruktur in Südostransdanubien. *AAH* 62 (2011) 1–28.

BRAASCH 2007
BRAASCH, O.: Gallipoli ahead – Air Survey between the Baltic and Mediterranean Sea. *ŠtZ* 41 (2007) 84–97.

DOMBAY 1939
DOMBAY, J.: *A zengővárkonyi őskori telep és temető.* (The Prehistoric Settlement and Cemetery at Zengővárkony). ArchHung 23. Budapest 1939.

DOMBAY 1959
DOMBAY, J.: Próbaásatás a villánykövesdi kőrézkori lakótelepen (Probegrabung an der aeneolithischen Ansiedlung bei Villánykövesd, Kom. Baranya). *JPMÉ* 1959 (1960) 55–75.

DOMBAY 1960
DOMBAY, J.: *Die Siedlung und das Gräberfeld von Zengővárkony.* ArchHung 37. Budapest 1960.

Kalicz 1983–1984

Kalicz, N.: Übersicht über den Forschungstand der Entwicklung der Lengyel-Kultur und die ältesten „Wehranlagen" in Ungarn. *MUAG* 33–34, (1983–1984) 271–293.

Kovárník 2003

Kovárník, J.: Jungneolithische und bronzezeitliche Kreisgrabenanlage in Mähren. In: Burdukiewicz, J. M. et al. (Hrsg.): *Erkenntnisjäger – Kultur und Umwelt des frühen Menschen. Festschrift für Deitrich Mania* (Veröffentlichung des Landesamtes für Archäologie Sachsen-Anhalt – Landesmuseum für Vorgeschichte 57/1) Halle/Saale 2003, 325–336.

Kuzma 2005

Kuzma, I.: Kruhuvé priekupové útvary na Slovensku – aktuálny stav (Kreisgrabenanlagen in der Slowakei – heutiger Forschungstand). In: Cheben, I. – Kuzma, I. (Hrsg.): *Otázky neolitu a eneolitu naših krajín 2004*. Archeologica Slovaka Monographiae – Communicationes 8. Bratislava 2005, 185–223.

Lengvári 2009

Lengvári, I.: Dombay János légifotói. In: Fazekas, F. (ed.): *Tanulmányok Visy Zsolt 65. születésnapjára*. Pécs 2009, 183–190.

Osztás – Marton – Sófalvi 2004

Osztás, A. – Marton, T. – Sófalvi, A.: Szólád-Kisaszó. In: Honti, Sz. et al.: A tervezett M7-es autópálya Somogy megyei szakaszának megelőző régészeti feltárása III (2002–2003). *SMK* 16 (2004) 61–62.

Melichar – Neubauer 2010

Melichar, P. – Neubauer, W. (Hrsg.): Mittelneolithische Kreisgrabenanlagen in Niederösterreich. *Mitteilungen der Prähistorischen Komission 7*. Wien 2010.

Somogyi 2007

Somogyi, K.: Die besonderen Grabenanlagen der Lengyel-Kultur in Kaposújlak-Várdomb-Dűlő im Komitat Somogy (SW-Ungarn). In: Kozłowski, J. K. – Raczky, P. (eds): *The Lengyel, Polgár and Related Cultures in the Middle/Late Neolithic in central Europe*. Kraków 2007, 329–344.

Petrasch 1990

Petrasch, J.: Mittelneolithische Kreisgrabenanlagen in Mitteleuropa. *BRGK* 71 (1990) 407–564.

Pusztai 1956

Pusztai, R.: A szemelyi kőrézkori ház [Das steinkupferzeitliche Haus von Szemely]. *AÉ* 83 (1956) 39–44.

Tokai 2008
Tokai, Z.-M.: 0711 Nagykanizsa-Palin–Anyagnyerőhely. http://www.zmmi.hu/gm/m7_kiadvany/Htm/031_0711.htm

Trnka 1991
Trnka, G.: Studien zu mittelneolithischen Kreisgrabenanlagen. *MPK* 26. Wien 1991.

Zalai-Gaál 1982
Zalai-Gaál, I.: A lengyeli kultúra a Dél-Dunántúlon [Die Lengyel-Kultur im südlichen Transdanubien]. *BÁMÉ* 10–11 (1982) 3–29.

Zalai-Gaál 1990
Zalai-Gaál, I.: A neolitikus körárokrendszerek kutatása a Dél-Dunántúlon (Die Erforschung der neolithischen Kreisgrabensysteme in SO-Transdanubien). *AÉ* 117 (1990) 3–24.

Zalai-Gaál 1990a
Zalai-Gaál, I.: Neue Daten zur Erforschung der spätneolithischen Schanzwerke im südlichen Transdaunbien. *Zalai Múzeum* 2 (1990) 31–46.

Zoffmann 1972–73
Zoffmann, Zs.: Die unveröffentlichten Pläne des neolithischen Gräberfeldes von Zengővárkony. *JPMÉ* 17–18 (1972–73) 47–50.

III. Prehistoric fortified settlements
Early Bronze Age earthworks

Besides the Neolithic enclosures, there is another distinctive group of the numerous earthworks and fortified sites discovered from the air in Baranya County. They belong to the Early Bronze Age, namely to the periods of the so-called Zók-Vučedol and Somogyvár-Vinkovci cultures (ca. 2500–2000 BC). Two fortified sites of this type had been known from excavation at Pécs–Nagyárpád and Zók (10 km west of Pécs).

These Early Bronze Ages sites have several common characteristics; they are all located at promontory-like places, near the end of elongated hills that are formed by the confluence of streams. All of the sites have several defensive works dividing an acropolis-like fortified centre at the end of a hill that overlooks stream-cut valleys.

At many of the fortified settlement sites described here we found surface finds belonging to various periods, such as the Copper Age, the Early Bronze Age, and the Late Bronze Age. However, there were some sites that produced only Early Bronze Age material (such as Szemely–Felső-rét and Peterd–Bakaszó). The Szemely–Felső-rét site provided the most valuable information in this respect: both our field-walking and the motorway excavation that cut the edge of the site produced only Early Bronze Age finds.

These single-date sites, together with the fact that Early Bronze Age finds were present at each and every other site in question, allow the conclusion that

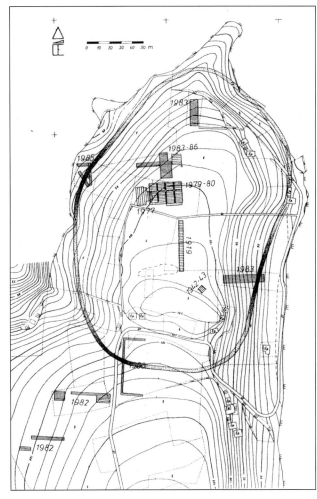

III.1: Map of the Zók–Várhegy fortified settlement (after ECSEDY 1999)

irrespective of other dates, the fortifications were extant at least during the Early Bronze Age period.

The finds most characteristic of the Early Bronze Age material recovered are vessel sherds adorned with encrusted patterns[1] on the inside as well as roughly brushed or in some cases pinched decoration. These stray finds, however, do not allow a more specific dating.

---

1   At the sites Szemely–Felső-rét, Pécsudvard–Bab-föld, and Görcsönydoboka–Erdő-föld, we found these type of bowls with encrustation both on the inside and the outside: G. Kulcsár dates this type to the Somogyvár-Vinkovci period (KULCSÁR 1997, 118–119).

III.2: Aerial photograph of Zók–Várhegy (B. G. 21. 04. 2013)

III.3: Distribution of the Early Bronze Age fortified settlements in the vicinity of Pécs

Fortified settlements of similar structure are also known from the eponymous site of the Late Copper Age–Early Bronze Age Vučedol culture[2] in Croatia as well as from Zók–Várhegy[3] in Baranya County. Croatian research expects more of these sites to be discovered along the Danube River.[4]

Gábor Bándi gave a fairly detailed description about the structure of the fortified settlement he excavated at Pécs–Nagyárpád-Dióstető. According to Bándi's observations the settlement lay on a promontorial hilltop[5] that was fortified by a linear ditch that isolated the site from the rest of the plateau, and it had a separate, acropolis-like fortified part. He dated the site to the Somogyvár-Vinkovci Culture without doubt. Gyula Nováki has also reported on a site of similar layout from Nagygörbő–Várhegy[6], (Northern Transdanubia), and Zsuzsa Miklós from Döbrököz–Tüszküs[7] (Tolna County), a site that also shows up in Google Earth satellite imagery. We know only of short descriptions in the literature of the Early Bronze Age fortified settlements at Oltárc–Márki-hegy and Galambok–Öreg-hegy.[8]

The eponymous Early Bronze Age Somogyvár–Kupavár-hegy site is also located on a flat-topped promontory hill surrounded by steep slopes on three sides.[9] Comparing these formerly known sites with the information we derived from remote sensing and field walking data there seems to be a nearly even distribution of these Early Bronze Age fortified sites in the hilly areas of the Transdanubian region.[10]

Thus far we have not had the opportunity to examine in detail the fortified sites we have discovered. However, the aerial photographs and field-walking data already allow for several conclusions to be drawn about them. It appears that the settlement structure of the Early Bronze Age in our region was far more complex than was previously suspected. In certain areas we can identify a dense network of fortified centres, but we also managed to find several smaller, unfortified settlements between these centres.

The fortified Early Bronze Age sites near Pécs form an approximately evenly spaced network – they are located at distances of 5 to 7 kilometres from each other, all of them are built on similar geographical features. The network appears to be approximately regular with small differences in distances caused by natural irregularities in the terrain. Though only hypothetical, the observation regarding the way that these sites are located was enough to predict the location of three previously unknown fortified Early Bronze Age settlements (Bogád, Pereked and Peterd) simply by creating intersecting buffer zones around the known sites.

---

2   SCHMIDT 1945.
3   ECSEDY 1983.
4   TASIĆ 1992.
5   BÁNDI 1979, 64. Unfortunately, he never published the plan of his excavations.
6   NOVÁKI 1965, 169, Fig. 2.
7   MIKLÓS 1997, 60–63, Figs 41–24.
8   HORVÁTH 1994, 97.
9   HONTI 1994, 5–6, Fig. 1.
10   A KULCSÁR 2009, 264–268. gives a summary of Somogyvár-Vinkovci settlement sites.

Catalogue

1. Boda–North of Alsó Kaposi út

Location: east of the village of Boda, on the promontorial end of a plateau
Entire area: at least 1.8 ha
Number of defensive ditches: 2 (possibly 3)
Orientation: north-south

Description: We identified the site in satellite imagery. The subsequent field-walking produced Early Bronze Age pottery. The defences of the settlement are only partially visible; two distinct and a possible outer, faint linear anomaly can be discerned in the images. Similarly to the Olasz site, there may be remains of ramparts in the forest that covers the slope to the north of the enclosure. Though only few details of this site have shown up so far, its main characteristics suggest that it belongs to the group of Early Bronze Age fortified settlements.
Sources: satellite images, aerial photographs, field-walking
Date: Early Bronze Age

III.5: Satellite image of the promontory separated from the plateau by multiple ditches revealed as cropmarks (07. 11. 2004)

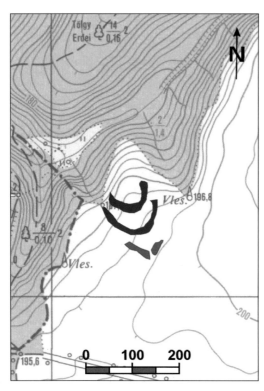

III.4: Plan of the defences of the Boda settlement

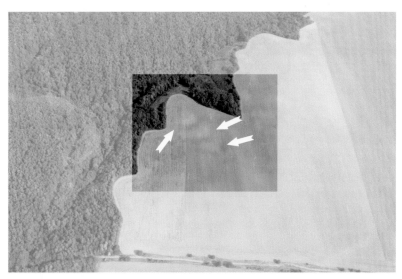

III.6: Aerial photograph of the Boda site
(B. G. – G. Cs. 16. 09. 2011)

2. Bogád–End of Krúdy Gy. Street

Location: east of the village of Bogád, northwest of the field called Venyet-dűlő, on the top of a 15–20 m high hill that gently slopes towards a stream to its north
Area of the "acropolis": partially visible, complete area cannot be measured
Entire area: cannot be determined exactly; at least 3–4 ha
Number of defensive ditches: 3+1 outer
Orientation: north-south

Description: In a Google Earth satellite image taken in 2007, three curved, parallel soilmarks show up, together with some pits. A fourth, outlying linear cropmark blocks the end of the hill from the south. In the area between the outer and the inner ditches, we found a few uncharacteristic, but most likely Early Bronze Age pottery sherds.
Sources: satellite images, aerial photographs, field-walking
Date: most probably Early Bronze Age

III.7: Map of the Bogád fortified settlement based on satellite images and aerial photographs

III.8: Satellite image of the multiple defensive ditches on the hill at the southwestern edge of the village of Bogád (soilmarks, 07. 11. 2004)

*III.9: Aerial photograph
of the Bogád fortified settlement
(B. G. – G. Cs. 07. 05. 2011)*

3. Görcsönydoboka–Erdő-föld

Location: north of the village of Görcsönydoboka, on the northern tip of a wide plateau gently sloping towards the south
Area of the "acropolis": 1 ha (estimated)
Entire area: 3 ha (estimated)
Number of defensive ditches: 2
Orientation: north-south

Description: An oval, partially visible enclosure showed up during aerial survey. Its northern part is likely to be covered by the forest on the slope. The surface finds that include a vessel sherd with encrusted decoration on its inner surface dated the site Early Bronze Age.
Sources: aerial photographs, satellite images, field-walking
Date: Early Bronze Age, probably Somogyvár-Vinkovci culture

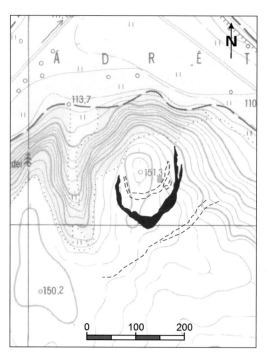

III.10: Map of the defensive ditches of Görcsönydoboka

III.11: Satellite image of the fortified settlement near Görcsönydoboka (24. 03. 2006)

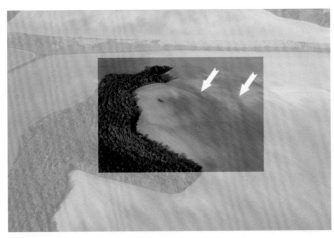

III.12: Aerial photograph of the Görcsönydoboka–Erdő-föld site (B. G. 27. 04. 2007)

4. Olasz–Olaszi-hegy

Location: west of the village of Olasz, on a northward extension of a plateau that overlooks the valley of a stream
Area of the "acropolis": ca. 2 ha
Entire area: ca. 9.6 ha
Number of defensive structures: 2 ditches on the south; 2 main rows of ramparts on the northern and western slopes.
Orientation: north-south

Description: A double and a single ditch on the plateau show up in aerial photography. Thick forest covers the northern tip of the plateau; joining the previously mentioned ditches, two rows of ramparts show up in the filtered 2012 LiDAR survey data of the forested area. This link between the ditches and the ramparts suggests that the ramparts belong to the Early Bronze Age fortified settlement, partially confirmed by surface finds.
Sources: aerial photographs, field-walking, satellite image, LiDAR survey
Date: the fortified settlement is likely to be of Early Bronze Age date. However, concentrations of Copper Age and Late Bronze Age surface finds have also been identified on the site

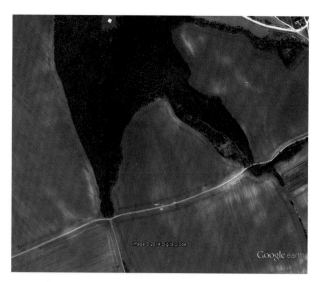

Ill.14: The Olasz–Olaszi-hegy site shown in a satellite image (18. 03. 2012)

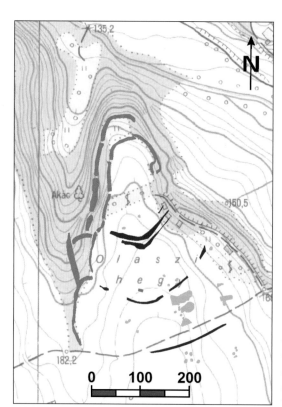

Ill.13: Map of the Olasz Bronze Age earthwork based on aerial photographs and LiDAR data. In the LiDAR image, the ramparts are marked in brown. In the aerial photographs, the excavation trenches are marked in grey.

III.15: Aerial photograph of Olasz–Olaszi-hegy fortified settlement (B. G. 07. 11. 2007)

III.16a: Shaded relief map of the Olasz–Olaszi-hegy site based on LiDAR data

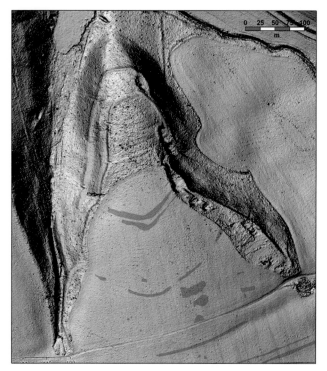

III.16b: A composite plan of ramparts detected in LiDAR data (green) and trenches visible in aerial photographs (blue)

5. Pécsudvard–Bab-föld

Location: south of the village of Pécsudvard, at the southern tip of an elongated hill bordered by two confluent streams
Area of the "acropolis": ca. 1 ha
Entire area: at least 3.5 ha (6 ha within the supposed third defensive ditch)
Number of defensive ditches: 2 (possibly 3)
Orientation: south-north

Description: Showing up in places as double ditched, an oval enclosure has been detected during several aerial surveys near the southern end of the hill. Located 45 and 280 m from the enclosure, at least one, but possibly two linear ditches separate the southern part of the hill from the rest of the plateau. The surface finds date to several archaeological periods from the Early Bronze Age up to the Late Bronze Age. The Late Bronze Age finds appeared to be concentrated on the northeastern part of the site, around the benchmark with a height of 163.1 m, but few of them also were found on other parts of the settlement. The majority of the Early Bronze Age finds were found in and around the oval enclosure in the southern part of the site, and between the enclosure and the linear ditches. Some were also found north of the defensive works.
Sources: JPM Archive, aerial photographs and satellite images, field-walking
Literature: BÁNDI – PETRES – MARÁZ 1979, 71, Site no. 26 (Babos-dűlő)
Date: Early Bronze Age, Late Bronze Age

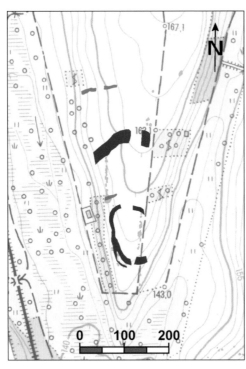

III.17: Plan of the Pécsudvard–Bab-föld fortified settlement

III.18: Pécsudvard–Bab-föld: two views of the site in satellite imagery (23. 09. 2007)

III.19: Aerial photograph of the Pécsudvard–Bab-föld site, with trenches that are mentioned in the description (13. 02. 2008)

6. Pereked–Alsó-mező

Location: on the edge of a loess plateau overlooking the present-day village of Pereked
Entire area: 6 ha
Area of the "acropolis": 1.4 ha including the defensive works; inner area: 0.6 ha
Number of defensive ditches: 3+1
Orientation: north-south

Description: The acropolis was established by digging three defensive ditches on a northward extending part of the edge of the loess plateau. Another defensive line was constructed 110–130 m to the south of the central fortification. Our field-walking produced mostly untypical pottery finds, some of which may be dated to the Early and Middle Bronze Age.
Sources: aerial photographs and satellite imagery, field-walking
Date: Early Bronze Age, Middle Bronze Age (Transdanubian Encrusted Pottery culture)

III.22: Satellite image showing the Pereked–Alsó-mező site (05. 02. 2007)

III.21: Plan of the Pereked–Alsó-mező site

← *III.20: Aerial photograph of the Pécsudvard–Bab-föld site (13. 02. 2008)*

7. Peterd–Bakaszó

Location: north of the village of Peterd, on a hill surrounded on three sides by two confluent streams
Entire area: 6.5 ha
Area of the "acropolis": partially visible, ca. 1.8–2 ha
Number of defensive ditches: 2
Orientation: south-north

Description: Satellite images and aerial photographs show a smaller, partially enclosed area near the tip of the plateau lying ca. 20 m above two confluent streams. 150–170 m to the south, another curved ditch blocks the entrance to the triangular, promontory-like plateau. On the eastern and western side of the plateau, the slope is steep and there is no sign of a ditch. There is a linear feature, possibly the trace of a street, defined by a north-south oriented soilmark that seems to connect the two main ditches (cf. G. Bándi's description of a similar feature at the Nagyárpád site[11]). We found characteristic Early Bronze Age pottery during our field-walking.
Sources: aerial photographs and satellite imagery, field-walking
Date: Early Bronze Age

III.24: Satellite image of the Peterd–Bakaszó site

III.23: Plan of the Peterd–Bakaszó fortified settlement

---

11   BÁNDI – PETRES – MARÁZ 1979, 64.

III.25: Aerial photograph of the Peterd–Bakaszó site
(B. G. – G. Cs. 31. 05. 2012)

III.26: Infrared photo of Peterd–Bakaszó (B. G. – G. Cs. 11. 05. 2012)

*III.27: Infrared photo
of Peterd–Bakaszó
(B. G. – G. Cs. 11. 05. 2012)*

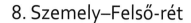

8. Szemely–Felső-rét

Location: north of the village of Szemely, on the southern tip of a hill flanked by two valleys that meet on the south side of the hill

Entire area: 4.5 ha of the enclosed settlement, there were also unenclosed features to the north of the structure

Area of the "acropolis": the enclosed area is 1.2 ha; the whole structure, including the triple defences, extends to 2 ha

Number of defensive ditches: 3

Orientation: south-north

Description: Surrounded by multiple ditches and a palisade, an enclosure 180×145 m in size lies 15 m above the valley that encircles the south end of the hill. To the north, two additional, linear ditches cut off the south part of the hill. The site is likely to be identical with the site named Szemely–Poljanak–Törökdomb in the gazetteer of the Early Bronze Age Somogyvár-Vinkovci culture sites by G. Bándi.

Sources: aerial photographs and satellite imagery, field-walking, literature

Literature: Bándi – Petres – Maráz 1979, 71, Site no.33

Date: There is an extensive area with Early Bronze Age finds in the cultivated land called Felső-rét. Finds and features belonging to the same period (Somogyvár-Vinkovci culture) were found during the recent M60 Motorway rescue excavations (site no. B082) that cut the northern edge of the site.[12]

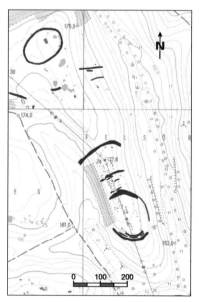

III.28: Plan of the Szemely–Felső-rétek site

---

[12]   Zsolt I. Tóth, pers. comm.

III.29: Aerial photograph of the Szemely–Felső-rétek site with the motorway rescue excavation (B. G. 07. 11. 2007)

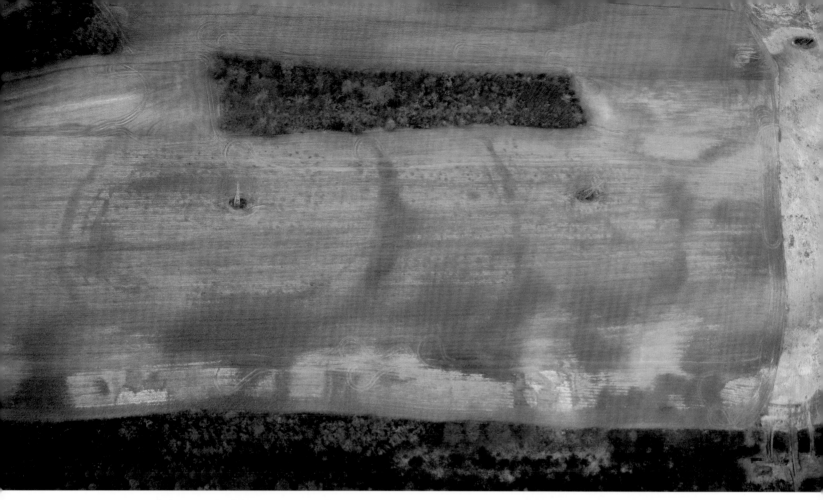

III.30: Aerial photograph of the Szemely–Felső-rétek fortified settlement. The numerous pits between the defensive works are clearly visible. (B. G. 07. 11. 2007)

III.31: Trace of the ditches of the Szemely–Felső-rétek fortified settlement seen from ground level

III.32: Szemely–Felső-rétek: photo of an excavated Early Bronze Age pit (courtesy of Zsolt Tóth)

III.33: Registered finds from the Szemely–Felső-rétek motorway rescue excavation (excavation of Zsolt Tóth, photos by T. S. A.)

9. Szilvás–Ó-szeg

Location: south-southwest of the village of Szilvás, on the eastern side of a plateau surrounded on three sides by the valleys of two confluent streams
Area of the "acropolis": 4.5 ha, with an annex of 4.5 ha attached to it by an adjoined ditch
Entire area: the area of the plateau cut off by the northernmost ditch is 22.7 ha
Number of defensive ditches: 3 (possibly 5)
Orientation: southeast-northwest

Description: 300×200 m in size, the "acropolis" of the Szilvás settlement is much larger than average. The earthwork lies on the eastern edge of a plateau 15–20 m in height overlooking a stream valley. An annex can be discerned on the western and northern side of the acropolis. Cutting off the rest of the plateau to the north, two linear cropmarks – possible ditches – running west-east are visible in aerial photographs. We found Early Bronze Age surface finds on the site. Though the general layout and the size of this site is somewhat different from the rest of the Early Bronze Age fortified settlements presented in this volume, we list it here based on its main characteristics.
Sources: aerial photographs and satellite imagery, field-walking
Date: Early Bronze Age

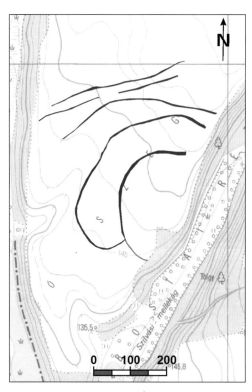

III.34: Plan of the Szilvás–Ó-szeg ditches

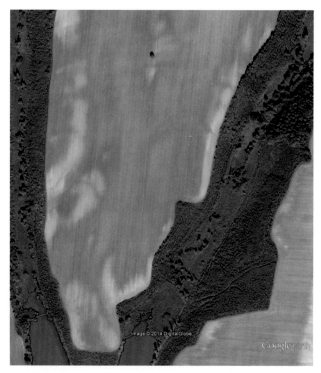

III.35: Satellite image of the Szilvás–Ó-szeg defensive works (23. 09. 2007)

118

III.36: Aerial photograph of the Szilvás–Ó-szeg site (B. G. 11. 06. 2011)

Literature

BÁNDI – PETRES – MARÁZ 1979
BÁNDI, G. – PETRES, É. F. – MARÁZ, B.: Baranya megye az őskorban. Korai bronzkor – Somogyvár-Vinkovci kultúra. In: Bándi, G. (ed.): *Baranya megye története az őskortól a honfoglalásig*. Pécs 1979, 59–73.

ECSEDY 1983
ECSEDY, I.: Ásatások Zók-Várhegyen (1971–1982). (Előzetes jelentés). *JPMÉ* 17 (1983) 59–105.

ECSEDY 1999
ECSEDY, I.: *Zók-Várhegy: egy szőlőhegy évezredei*. Zók 1999.

HONTI 1994
HONTI, Sz.: A mészbetétes kerámia kultúrája leletei Somogyvárról. *SMK* 10 (1994) 5–21.

HORVÁTH 1994
HORVÁTH, L.: Nagykanizsa és környékének története az újkőkortól a római kor végéig. In: Rózsa, Gy. (ed.): *Nagykanizsa története I.* Nagykanizsa 1994, 85–141.

KULCSÁR 1997
KULCSÁR, G.: Kora bronzkori belső díszes tálak a Dunántúlon. *Savaria – A Vas Megyei Múzeumok értesítője* 24/3 (1997) 115–140.

KULCSÁR 2009
KULCSÁR, G.: *The beginnings of the Bronze Age in the Carpathian Basin*. Varia archaeologica Hungarica 23. Budapest 2009.

MIKLÓS 2007
MIKLÓS, Zs.: *Tolna megye várai*. Varia archaeologica Hungarica 22. Budapest 2007.

NOVÁKI 1965
NOVÁKI, Gy.: A Nagygörbő-Várhegy-i korabronzkori erődített telep. *AÉ* 92 (1965) 168–175.

TASIĆ 1992
TASIĆ, N.: Das Modell befestigter Siedlungen der Vučedol-Kultur im jugoslawischen Donaugebiet (Vučedol, Belegiš). In: Aspes, A. (Hrsg.): *Settlement Patterns between the Alps and the Black Sea 5th to 2nd Millenium B.C.* Symposium, Verona – Lazise 1992. Verona 1995, 111–118.

SCHMIDT 1945
SCHMIDT, R. R.: *Die Burg Vučedol*. Zagreb 1945.

IV. Mounds in the forest, cropmarks in the field
Remains of the Iron Age in Baranya County

The Pécs–Jakab-hegy hillfort

Located to the northwest of Pécs, the Jakab-hegy (Jakab Hill) has been known as an archaeological site since the 19th century. Even the earliest publication dates its main features, a hillfort and a barrow cemetery, to the Iron Age and to the Copper Age.[1] The first documented archaeological excavation at the site took place in 1948, when Gyula Török excavated 9 burial mounds. The most important finds he recovered from one of the tumuli were a bi-metallic dagger with a bronze hilt with openwork decoration and iron blade, and horse harness fittings.[2]

Led by Borbála Maráz, the excavations continued between 1976 and 1983. She unearthed 32 barrows and cross-sectioned the ramparts of the hillfort at several places.[3] Simultaneously with B. Maráz's investigations, Gábor Kárpáti excavated the Pauline monastery located in the centre of the plateau on the top of Jakab-hegy.

Unfortunately, B. Maráz has to date published only some preliminary reports on the find material. According to her observations, there were Late Bronze Age finds both underlying the tumuli and in the material of the ramparts. These finds seem to have belonged to the earliest settlers of the mountain.[4] A bronze hoard found on the site may be indicative of the richness of the Late Bronze Age settlement.

It seems likely that the ramparts (or at least parts of them) were raised during the same period when the barrow cemetery was in use. The excavations showed that the tumuli had an approximately uniform structure: the mounds were ringed by stones. The burnt remains of the deceased and the grave goods put on the pyre were placed in a simple or stone-lined cist in the middle. The tumuli can be dated to the 8th–7th centuries BC.[5]

There are stray finds that indicate the use of the site in the Late Iron Age Celtic and the Early Imperial Roman period.[6] Our field-walking also indicates that the mountain was inhabited during the Roman times: we recovered iron fibulae, nails, a key, and a 2nd century AD coin, a sestertius of Faustina, the wife of Marcus Aurelius.

B. Maráz estimated the number of tumuli on the mountain to be 300. However, to completely survey the cemetery using ground-based methods is a very difficult task for several reasons: forest cover attenuates the GPS signals, and also causes reduced visibility that renders a conventional

---

1 HORVÁTH 1871, 61–62.
2 TÖRÖK 1950.
3 MARÁZ 1979.
4 MARÁZ 1985–86. Gy. Török also mentions Middle Bronze Age encrusted pottery sherds from the mountain (TÖRÖK 1950, 4).
5 MARÁZ 1996.
6 MARÁZ 2008, 69–70.

geodetic survey extremely time-consuming and laborious. Furthermore, the thick undergrowth hides the less prominent tumuli during most of the year.

It seems therefore that under such circumstances, airborne laser scanning (ALS/LiDAR) is the most effective of the recently available methods to achieve a complete survey of the still extant archaeological remains. In March 2012, just before the beginning of the growing season, we had the Jakab-hegy surveyed with LiDAR.

In the terrain model we acquired by processing the point cloud data, we could detect several known and formerly unknown features, e.g.:

- It turned out that there is an outer annex attached to the main line of the ramparts of the so-called acropolis at the south-eastern end of the hillfort.
- The acropolis also has an inner, partially extant rampart near the hill-top.
- Numerous tumuli, both intact and excavated, are clearly distinguishable and therefore can be mapped in front of the western tract of the larger ramparts.
- It has been known that on the western side there are two rows of ramparts starting from the south-western corner gate. However, at this location, only the south-western section of the outer rampart was distinguishable. The LiDAR survey made it clear that the outer rampart runs along the entire western wall, and – following the main line – it turns east and continues along the larger rampart up to the north gate
- Based on the LiDAR data, all the former excavations and backfilled gates in the ramparts can be exactly located and mapped, though it seems that there were no gates that were not previously known.

Aside from the ramparts and the tumuli, remains of the Pauline monastery and the adjoining walls, towers, and other features are also clearly visible in the LiDAR data. It seems likely that the defensive wall had a previously unknown section around the northwestern corner of the compound.

The late 18th century First Military Ordnance Survey map of the area depicts three larger tumuli near the village of Kővágótöttös at the southern foot of Jakab-hegy. The Second Military Ordnance Survey map (mid-19th century) shows only two of them. Around 1950, Gy. Török reported eight tumuli in the area. He excavated one of them. He describes the structure of the barrow as being constructed of a 2 m thick layer of stones covered by earth of the same thickness. However, his report suggests that he did not entirely excavate the feature.[7]

Shadow-marks in aerial photographs taken in 2005 under snowy conditions show the three tumuli also visible in the previously mentioned earlier maps.[8] The LiDAR survey data indicate four tumuli for certain, and another one or two possible barrows to the west of them, in an area covered by thick vegetation. We have not yet managed to identify all the eight tumuli mentioned by Gy. Török. We surveyed the largest of the still extant tumuli using magnetometry and ground penetrating radar. The magnetometer survey covered a grid 50×50 m in size. The diameter of the barrow is ca. 20 m. Both methods revealed new details, but they did not provide a clear picture of the inner structure of the mound. However, the survey data may still serve as starting point for future investigations of the

---

7 TÖRÖK 1950, 5.
8 Showing signs of disturbance, the barrow excavated by Gy. Török is likely to be the northernmost one, now covered by vegetation.

barrow. In somewhat "noisy" data, a quadrangular anomaly and a trace of a possible inner structure showed up in the middle of the barrow in the magnetometer survey. Another one or perhaps two smaller internal features also became visible, that might be interpreted as traces of a pyre or a smaller, perhaps stone structure. It seems that the barrow was outlined by two circular features, possibly ditches or remains of stone circles, whose analogies were found at the tumuli on top of the Jakab-hegy.

The ground penetrating radar survey area was 30×30 m in size. At a depth of ca. 80 cm, the circular features and the roughly quadrangular, central magnetometer anomaly (a possible chamber) that showed up in the magnetogram also appeared as radar anomalies. Since the radar anomalies are not very distinct, they mostly show a phase shift, and not as differences in signal strength, they are not likely be of solid stone construction.

Open settlement complex near the village of Szajk

Carried out as part of the motorway construction works between 2005 and 2008 on the outskirts of the villages of Szajk and Babarc, several excavation campaigns[9] revealed parts of an extensive settlement complex that belongs to the Iron Age (6th–3rd centuries BC) later than that of the Jakab-hegy remains. The settlement extends to three hills divided by nearly parallel, north-south running stream valleys. Aerial surveys of the site in 2012 revealed numerous cropmark features both to the north and to the south of the excavated part of the settlement on the hill in the centre.[10] By mosaicing several infrared and normal colour aerial photographs, we could create a detailed picture of most parts of the site, though it cannot be determined presently that all the groups of features belong to the same Iron Age settlements or to different periods.

To enhance the results of the excavations and the aerial surveys, we carried out a magnetometer survey south of the excavated area. Here we had not been able to detect any features from the air, even though the distribution of excavated features made their presence possible. The magnetic survey provided valuable information and complemented the information gained through other methods.

Summing up the results, it seems likely that the Iron Age settlement consisted of small groups of rectangular, sunken-floor houses and associated pits. We have not been able to determine the date of the large pit west of the features in the magnetogram as yet, but considering the analogies from the neighbouring settlements, it may have served as a clay pit.

---

9   GÁBOR 2009; GÁTI 2009.
10   Interestingly, we found only very scarce traces of the other two settlements outside the excavated areas, though they certainly extended beyond the track of the motorway.

Literature

GÁBOR 2009
GÁBOR, O.: Kr. e. 5. századi oinochoé korsók Szajkról (Baranya megye). *JPMÉ* 50–52 (2005–2007) 66–83.

GÁTI 2009
GÁTI, Cs.: A szajki vaskori telep kulturális kapcsolatai. In: *MΩMOΣ 6. Őskoros Kutatók VI. Összejövetelének konferenciakötete.* Szombathely 2009, 65–79.

HORVÁTH 1871
HORVÁTH, A.: Pécsvidéki s egyéb leletek. *AK* 8 (1871) 60–62.

MARÁZ 1979
MARÁZ, B.: Pécs–Jakabhegy. Előzetes jelentés az 1976–1977. évi ásatásokról – Pécs–Jakabhegy. Vorbericht über die Ausgrabungen des Jahres 1976–1977. *AÉ* 106 (1979) 78–93.

MARÁZ 1985–86
MARÁZ, B.: Későbronzkori magaslati település Pécs–Jakabhegyen (Előzetes közlemény az 1976–83. évi ásatásokról) (Excavation on Pécs–Jakabhegy 1976–83. The Late Bronze Age settlement. Preliminary Report). *JPMÉ* 30–31 (1985-86) 39–64.

MARÁZ 1996
MARÁZ, B.: Pécs–Jakabhegy – Ausgrabungsergebnisse und die Fragen der Frühhallstattkultur in Südostpannonien. In: Jerem, E. – Lippert, A. (eds): *Die Osthallstattkultur. Akten des Internationalen Symposiums, Sopron, 10–14. Mai 1994,* Archeolingua 7. Budapest 1996, 255–267.

MARÁZ 2008
MARÁZ, B.: Archäologische Angaben zur mittleren und späten LaTène-Zeit in Südosttransdanubien. *CommArchHung* (2008) 65–93.

TÖRÖK 1950
TÖRÖK, GY.: A Pécs–Jakabhegyi földvár és tumulusok. *Arch Ért* 77 (1950) 4–7.

IV.1: Aerial photograph of the Pécs–Jakab-hegy hillfort (G. Cs. 13. 11. 2010)

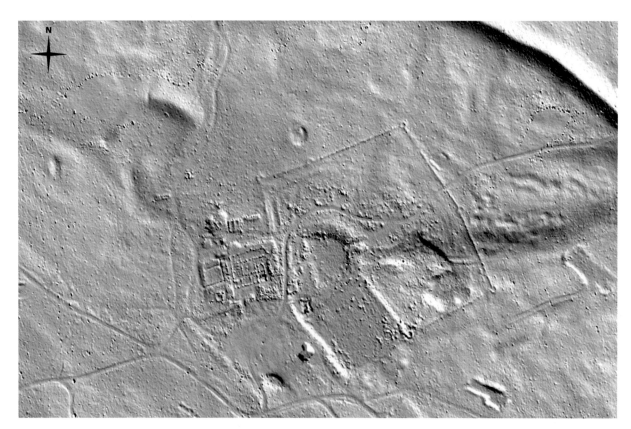

IV.2: A detail of Fig. IV.4 showing the area of the Pauline monastery

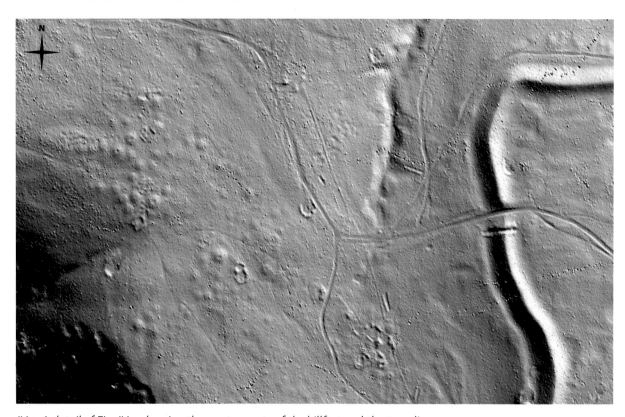

IV.3: A detail of Fig. IV.4 showing the western gate of the hillfort and the tumuli

a

IV.5: A bimetallic dagger found in one of the tumuli

b

c

IV.6: Roman coin found inside
the hillfort during our field-walking in 2011
(photo: Zsolt Tóth)

IV.7 a, b, c: Restored pottery vessels
from the excavation of the barrow cemetery
(photo: István Füzi)

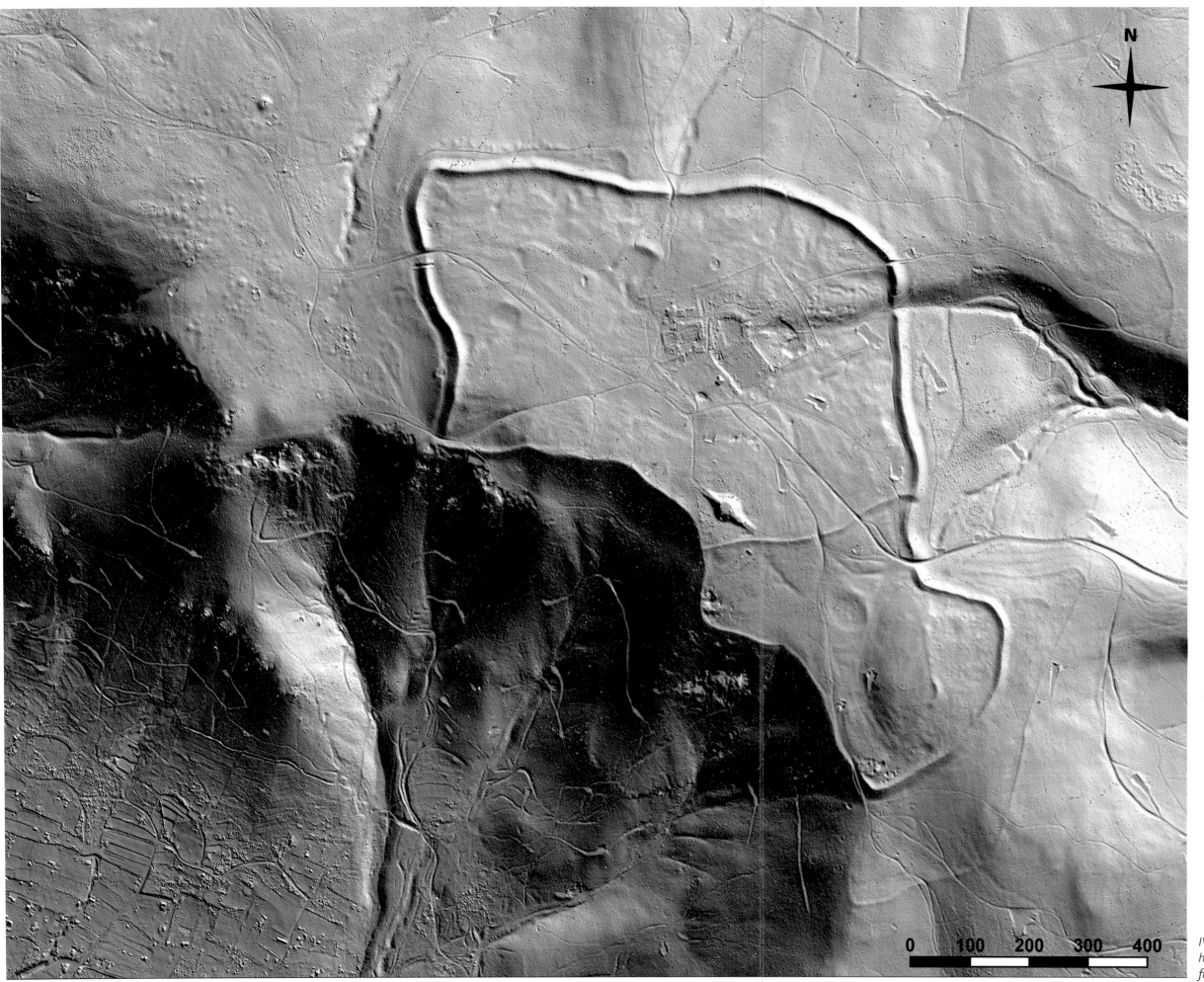

IV.4: LiDAR image of the Pécs–Jakab-hegy
hillfort and its surroundings with the vegetation
filtered out

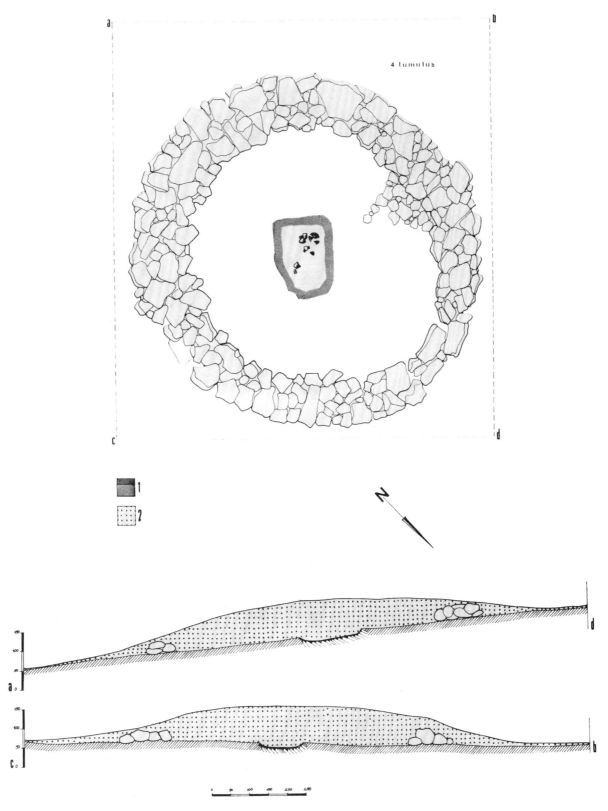

IV.8: Drawing showing one of the excavated tumuli (MARÁZ 1979, Abb 3)

IV.10: Shaded relief map of the Kővágótöttös tumuli based on filtered LiDAR data (a), an oblique view of the shaded relief map of the Kővágótöttös tumuli based on filtered LiDAR data (b)

← *IV.9: Aerial photograph of the tumuli near Kővágótöttös at the foot of Pécs–Jakab-hegy (B. G. – G. Cs. 02. 03. 2005)*

133

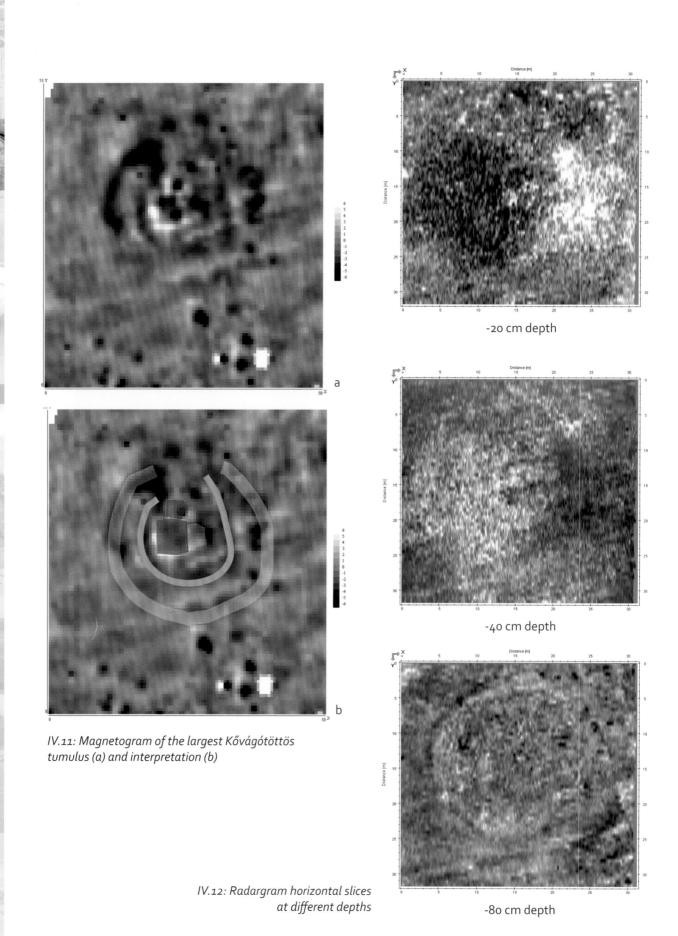

IV.11: Magnetogram of the largest Kővágótöttös tumulus (a) and interpretation (b)

IV.12: Radargram horizontal slices at different depths

-20 cm depth

-40 cm depth

-80 cm depth

IV.13: Excavated sunken-floor house of the Iron Age settlement near Szajk (excavation of Olivér Gábor, Photo: T. S. A.)

IV.14: Restored pottery from the Iron Age settlement near Szajk: (a-b) onichoé, (c) kantharos (excavation of Olivér Gábor, Photo: T. S. A.)

IV.15: Aerial photograph of the Iron Age settlement in the vicinity of the village of Szajk (B. G. – G. Cs. 21. 06. 2012)

IV.16: Infrared aerial photograph of the Szajk Iron Age settlement (B. G. – G. Cs. 21. 06. 2012)

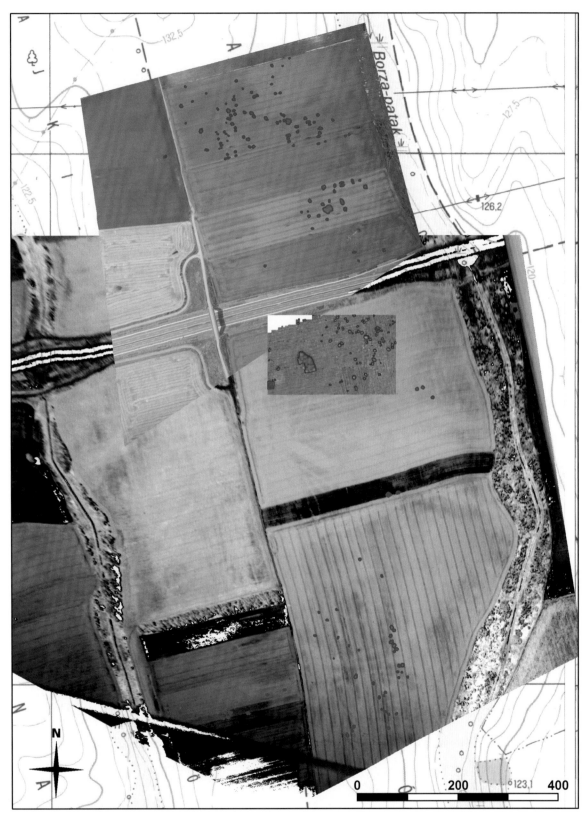

IV.17: A composite photo map using orthorectified aerial photographs taken in visible and infrared light, and the magnetic survey results

V. Invisible Villas
Traces of Roman settlements

Baranya County, being located in the former Roman province of Pannonia, has numerous Roman settlement sites. These range from small, rural settlements called *vici* made up of ephemeral building materials[1] to a large town called Sopianae. Between the two extremes, a type of settlement called *villa* was the most typical found in the rural landscape.[2] The *villae* were settlements of an agricultural nature with stables, workshops and granaries. They were located in the centre of estates and were places where the landowner stayed either permanently or temporarily. As a result, the owner's living quarters were in most cases at least as, if not more, comfortable than their urban counterparts. The buildings were made of stone or brick and included rooms heated in the winter by a hypocaust, mosaic floors, wall paintings, glazed windows and baths which were often in a separate building.

According to our present knowledge, the 10×3 km gently sloping periphery of the Jakab-hegy (west of Pécs – Sopianae) was one of the most densely populated areas in the Roman period. We know of at least three major *villa* settlements, traces of an aqueduct, and a number of smaller sites. The first of the three *villae,* located near Kővágószőlős, was excavated and restored for public display in the 1980s. The second *villa,* near the village of Cserdi in the western part of Kővágószőlős, was previously discovered from the air. It has been recently surveyed and excavated by archaeologists from the University of Pécs.[3]

This chapter describes the third *villa* at Bakonya–Csucsa-dűlő which is located between the Kővágószőlős and Cserdi estates. The site has been long known to be a Roman *villa*, based on surface finds, but has not been subject to detailed investigations.[4]

Our first flight over the site in 2006 revealed whitish areas against the brown ploughsoil. These were identified as the traces of ruined buildings whose limy building material had been mixed with the soil. When mapped, even these not so well-defined soil marks can be correlated with an elevated area in the terrain. This elevated area is surrounded on three sides by a series of curvilinear, silted depressions that form possible watercourses or streams which may have been active in the Roman period.

In 2008, cropmarks and shadow-marks revealed a much more detailed layout of the site. The layout included a *villa urbana* (dwelling house) 21×21 m in size with an atrium and apses, a 35×17 m wing attached to the northwest side of the villa, a bath house and a granary or storehouse 25.5×15.5 m

---

1   We have already discovered several settlements of the same type from the air, see: Bertók – Kovaliczky 2009.

2   The most significant excavations uncovering Roman *villae* in Baranya County: Komló–Mecsekjánosi-Közüzemi-völgy (Burger 1967), Babarc–Szabad-földek (Fazekas 2007, with further literature), Kővágószőlős (Burger 1978), Egerág–Kókapart (Pozsárkó 2000), Nagyharsány–Szárhegy (Fülep 1962; 1964), and recently Cserdi, see Footnote 2.

3   Szabó 2012, 2013.

4   Fülep – Burger 1979, 305, No. 8, Bakonya–Csucsai-dűlő.

in size with buttresses and a double row of columns. Amongst the buildings with nearly complete layouts, there are four (or possibly five) other partially discernible structures as well as the double linear traces of a road approaching the *villa* from the northwest.

In the summer of 2013, we performed a small-scale geophysical survey on the Bakonya *villa* as part of a Non-Invasive Archaeological Training School (NATS). We chose an area 60×40 m in size where cropmarks indicated the presence of a building, but without much detail. We set up the survey grid on the basis of an orthorectified aerial photograph. The magnetic survey proved the presence of the building and provided a detailed picture of its layout, thus contributing to our better knowledge of this complex site. The new data will also help to plan and make further research of the *villa* more effective.

The example of this site clearly demonstrates one of the cardinal rules of aerial archaeology, namely that a single flight over a site or an area is rarely enough. In this case, it took three years of repeated aerial photography to achieve a result that aids the planning of further research of the site in the most effective way.

Disregarding the Cserdi and Bakonya sites, the number of Roman settlements detected from the air in Baranya County is relatively low. Luckily, after eight years of unsuccessful aerial surveillance, we had the chance to record cropmarks of the buildings of a Roman *villa* site near the village of Szederkény during the previously mentioned summer training course. We already have finds and know of several archaeological features related to the *villa* settlement, such as a Late Roman cemetery, both from field-walking and from the rescue excavation that preceded the construction of the nearby motorway.

Literature

BERTÓK – KOVALICZKY 2009
BERTÓK, G. – KOVALICZKY, G.: Adalékok Baranya megye római kori településtörténetéhez. In: Fazekas, F. – Priskin, A. – Szabó, Á. (eds): *'Ripam omnem quaesivit' Ünnepi tanulmányok Visy Zsolt 65. születésnapjára tanítványaitól*. Specimina Nova Suppl. VIII. Pécs–Paks 2009.

BURGER 1967
BURGER, A. SZ.: Rómaikori villa maradványai Komló határában (Die Reste der Villa aus der Römerzeit in der Umgebung von Komló). *JPMÉ* (1967) 61–68.

BURGER 1978
BURGER, A. Sz.: The Roman Villa and Mausoleum at Kővágószőlős, near Pécs (Sopianae). Excavation 1977–1982 (Rómaikori villa és őskeresztény mauzóleum feltárása Kővágószőlősön 1977–1982). *JPMÉ* 30–31 (1987) 65–228.

FAZEKAS 2007
FAZEKAS, F. (Hrsg./Ed.): *Die römische Siedlung bei Babarc, Komitat Baranya/Ungarn – The Roman Settlement near Babarc, Baranya County/Hungary*. Passauer Universitätsschriften zur Archäologie 12. Rahden 2007.

FÜLEP 1962
FÜLEP, F.: Nagyharsány–Szárhegy. *RégFüz* 1/15 (1962) 32.

FÜLEP 1964
FÜLEP, F.: Nagyharsány–Szárhegy. *RégFüz* 1/17 (1964) 36.

FÜLEP – BURGER 1979
FÜLEP, F. – BURGER A. Sz.: Baranya megye a római korban. In: Bándi G.: *Baranya megye története az őskortól a honfoglalásig*. Pécs 1979, 223–328.

POZSÁRKÓ 2003
POZSÁRKÓ, Cs.: 113. Egerág, Kókapart. In: *Régészeti kutatások Magyarországon 2001*. Budapest 2003, 132–133.

SZABÓ 2012
SZABÓ, M.: Non-Invasive Methods in the Research of Pannonian Villas. In: *Hungarian Archaeology*, E-journal, 2012 Autumn.

SZABÓ 2013
SZABÓ, M.: Nem romboló régészeti módszerek alkalmazása a pannoniai villakutatásban. In: Bíró, Sz. – Vámos, P. (eds): *FiRKák II. Fiatal Római Koros Kutatók II. Konferencia kötete*, 2007. október 9–10. Visegrád, 2009. november 20–22. Komárom 2013, 493–502.

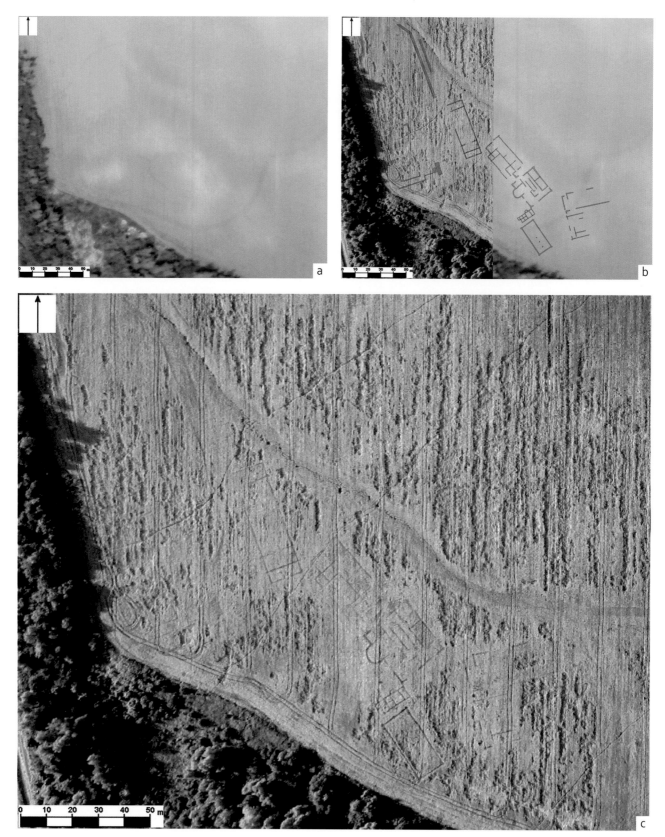

V.1: Aerial photographs of the Bakonya–Csucsa Roman villa taken under various crop conditions: (a) soilmark, (c) crops and (b) the different photos with the interpretation

V.2: Infrared photo showing the Bakonya–Csucsai-dűlő Roman villa (B. G. – G. Cs. 31. 05. 2012)

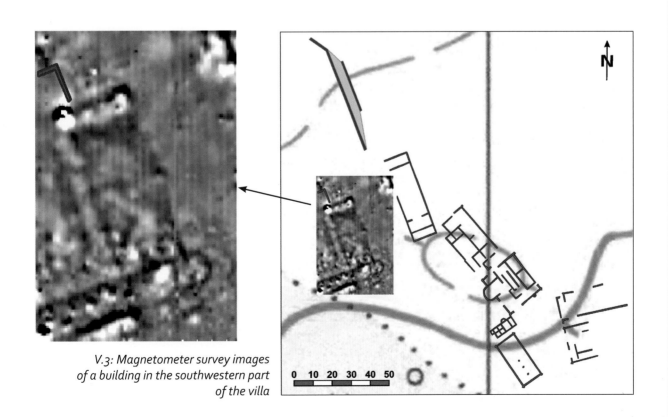

V.3: Magnetometer survey images of a building in the southwestern part of the villa

143

V.5: Aerial photograph of the Roman buildings near the village of Szederkény (B. G. – G. Cs.20. 06. 2013)

V.6: Roman Age cauldron from the motorway rescue excavation near the Szederkény villa (excavation of Gergely Kovaliczky, photo T. S. A.)

← *V.4: Aerial photograph of the Roman buildings near the village of Szederkény (NATS, Sz. M. 09. 06. 2013)*

VI. A church in the church?
Ground penetrating radar survey in and around Pécs Cathedral

Built during the 11th and 12th centuries AD, the current building of Pécs Cathedral is the result of major reconstructions in the 19th century. Only the main structural elements of the Cathedral remain relatively unaltered. An important, structurally unchanged element of the Cathedral is the Crypt and therefore it should be the focus of archaeological research. However, only small-scale rescue excavations could be made in the Crypt so far, and little is known about what may lie beneath its floor.

The first poorly documented "excavation" was devastating and took place in the Crypt on the orders of Gabriele Vecchi, general commander of Pécs following the town's retaking from the Ottomans in 1686.[1] To put it plainly, he had the tombs in the Crypt robbed and the valuables taken away. This is documented in letters of the contemporary Bishop of Pécs. Much later, in 1978, the archaeologist Mária G. Sándor led the first true rescue excavation in the northwest corner of the Crypt where she found remains of a Roman subsurface aqueduct and some graves.[2]

Evidence that General Vecchi was not thorough enough was proved by the results of the rescue excavation by the archaeologist Gábor Kárpáti in 1991. Aside from some undisturbed medieval graves, located next to the western wall, he managed to find the previously unknown grave of the best known Bishop of Pécs, Janus Pannonius. He was famous for being the first Renaissance poet and a successful politician of the mid-15th century Kingdom of Hungary. Kárpáti's excavation also provided new information on the structure of the building. He found that the pillars and columns that support the ceiling of the Crypt were placed on parallel foundation walls whose short sections he managed to identify in the 2 m wide excavation trench.[3] A subsequent small-scale excavation by G. Kárpáti and O. Gábor in 2001 revealed two empty medieval tombs.[4]

As can be seen from the excavations previously mentioned, excavation activity has been sporadic with no systematic research work having been carried out in the Crypt so far.

Ground penetrating radar survey

In 2008, we carried out a GPR survey of the area in front of the western façade of Pécs Cathedral at the request of the Bishopric and the local Bureau of Cultural Heritage Management. The reason for the request was the planned renovation of the cobblestone surface in front of the Cathedral, but, exploiting the situation, we asked for permission from the Bishop to survey the floor of the Crypt.

---

1   Boros 2000, 95, footnote 16.
2   Fülep – Burger 1981, 24–25; Fülep 1984, 55–57.
3   Kárpáti 1998, 2008.
4   Excavation report by Gábor Kárpáti, JPM Archive 2074–2007.

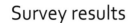

Survey results

The GPR survey of the Crypt proved that the short sections of foundation walls excavated by G. Kárpáti in 1991 indeed run under the floor across the entire length of the Crypt, thus supporting the pillars and columns. Complementing this information, the survey indicated that there may be a less substantial north-south orientated reinforcement connecting the parallel west-east oriented foundations of the pillars and columns.

Just under the flagstones of the floor east of the centre of the Crypt, there are anomalous GPR reflections indicating a rectangular, ca. 2.5×3 m feature. This anomaly is shown in the GPR radargram. According to the excavators, the anomaly can be correlated with one of the robbed tombs excavated in 2001. A similar anomaly can be seen in the centre of the Crypt, an obvious location for a tomb of a significant person or for relics of a holy person.

Strong GPR reflections were detected in the spaces between the previously mentioned parallel foundation walls indicating the remains of an underlying stone structure at a depth of ca. 100 cm. Though the exact plan of the structure could not be determined due to the medieval foundation walls that seem to overlie them, its location and depth makes it plausible to date it to the Roman period. Following this reasoning, the structure that underlies the Crypt is likely to be ecclesiastical in nature and is perhaps one of the burial chapels of the 4th–5th century Early Christian cemetery that surrounds the Cathedral site. In this case, only an excavation could prove the hypothesis.

Outside of the Cathedral

Ferenc Fülep of the Hungarian National Museum excavated part of the area in front of the western gate of the Cathedral in 1958. He uncovered the remains of a Roman aqueduct, the Early Christian Burial Chamber no. VII and the foundations of a north-south running medieval wall.[5]

The GPR survey correlates with the results of the former excavations also in the area in front of the western gate of the Cathedral. The area of the 1958 excavations of F. Fülep clearly shows up in the time slices made from the radar profiles as a difference in signal phase. The main structures, such as the previously mentioned Burial Chamber no. VII and the north-south oriented thick medieval wall are also visible as stronger reflections. The radar data, on the other hand, show that the unexcavated part of the medieval wall runs further north across the entire width of the square. Possibly being air-filled features, such as cisterns or crypts, two hitherto unknown features also appear in the northern part of the surveyed area.

---

5   FÜLEP 1984, 53–55, Fig.16a.

Literature

BOROS 2000
BOROS, L.: Adatgyűjtemény Janus Pannonius sírhelyének kérdéséhez. In: Bartók, I. – Jankovics, L. – Kecskeméti, G.: *Humanista műveltség Pannoniában*. Pécs 2000.

FÜLEP – BURGER 1981
FÜLEP, F. – BURGER, A. Sz.: *Pécs város régészeti topográfiája*. Kézirat, JPM Adattár. Budapest 1981.

FÜLEP 1984
FÜLEP, F.: *Sopianae*. ArchHung 50. Budapest 1984.

KÁRPÁTI 1998
KÁRPÁTI, G.: Hová temették Janus Pannoniust? Fél évezredes rejtély. *Pécsi Szemle* 1998/1, 21–27.

KÁRPÁTI 2008
KÁRPÁTI, G.: Janus Pannonius sírja. *JPMÉ* (2005–2007) 2008, 123–131.

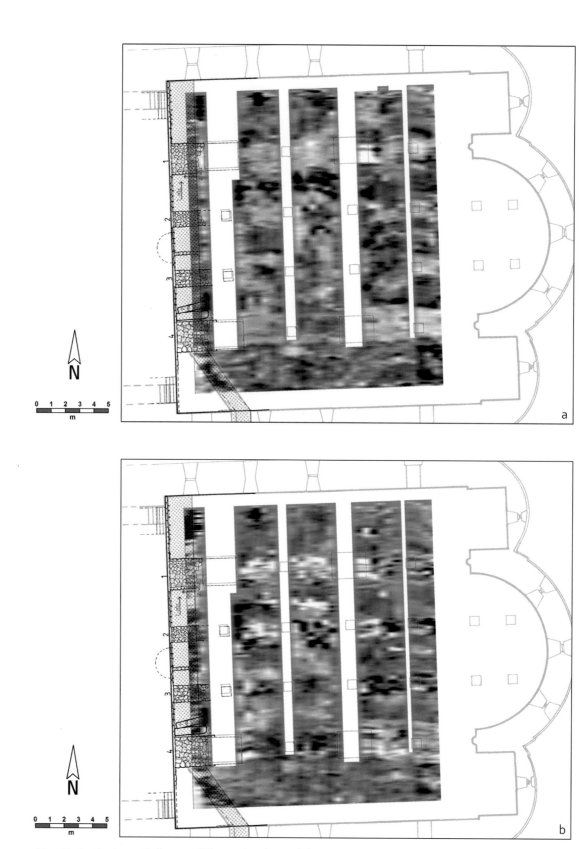

VI.1: Radar horizontal slices at different depths, and the interpretation of the survey in the Crypt of Pécs
Cathedral. (a) -6ocm (b) -8o cm (c) -100 cm (d) interpreted map

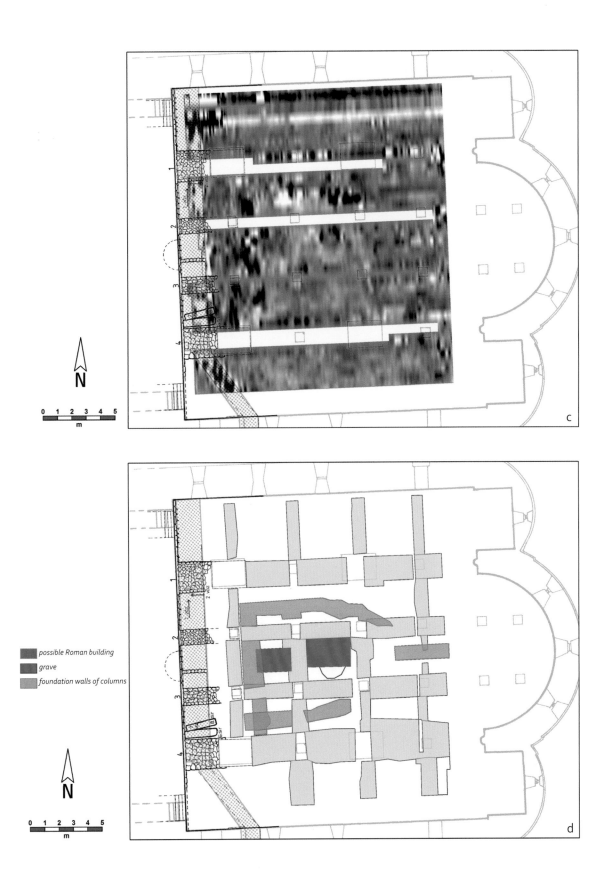

N

0 1 2 3 4 5
m

c

possible Roman building
grave
foundation walls of columns

N

0 1 2 3 4 5
m

d

151

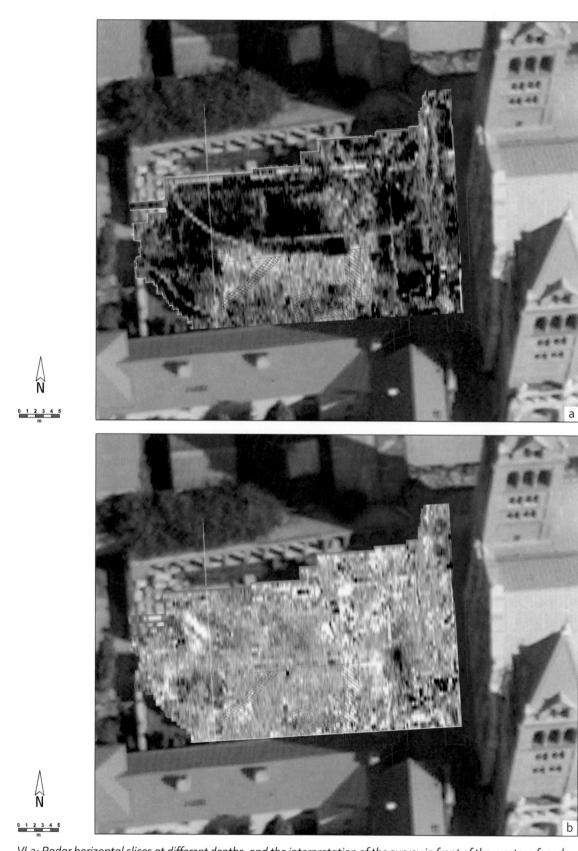

VI.2: Radar horizontal slices at different depths, and the interpretation of the survey in front of the western façade of Pécs Cathedral. (a) -60cm, (b) -80 cm, (c) -100 cm, (d) interpreted map (hatched areas: excavated features)

c

foundation wall
disturbed area
pipeline
electric cable
area excavated by F. Fülep
possible cavity

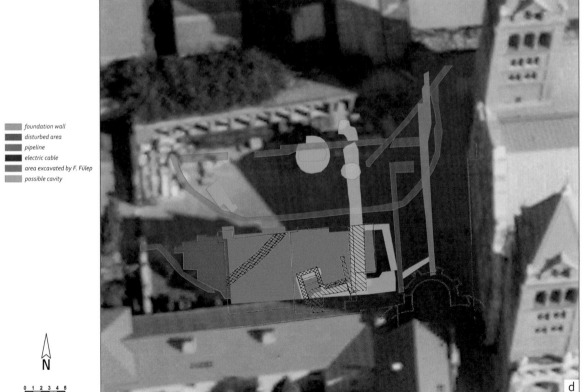

d

VII. A church under the ground
Ground penetrating survey in the village of Vokány

The medieval site of Trinitáspuszta ("Trinity" puszta) is located on the southern edge of Vokány. The area of the former co-operative farm is now privately owned and is still in agricultural use.

Literary sources[1]

This was the place, suggested by the site's name, where archaeologists suspected the location of a Benedictine abbey known from medieval literary sources. Though its date of foundation is unknown, it seems likely that the monastery, named after the Holy Trinity, was founded by the Siklósi branch of the Kán kindred. It is first mentioned in a charter dating to 1183 as *S. Trinitatis* when King Béla confirmed the donation of an estate by Pál of the Csák kindred at the request of Peter of the Kán family, bishop of Spalato (the present-day Split in Croatia) and Baya of the Zalók kindred.

According to charters issued in 1280, 1294, and 1303, the benefactors of the monastery were the Siklósi family. From 1240, the monastery was the seat of an abbot. In 1303, Péter of Siklós donated the monastery to the Cistercian order, and placed it under the supervision of the abbey of Heiligenkreutz in Austria. However, it seems likely that the Cistercian "rule" did not commence, or did not last long, since all the later sources mention the Benedictine order in relation to the monastery. In 1415, the abbot Tamás participated in the Council of Constance.

County officials often held their meetings and days of jurisdiction in the settlement named after the monastery. In 1475, Pope Sixtus IV appointed Antal, the bishop of Megara, *commendator*, i.e. the honorary abbot, of Szent Trinitás. Similar to the date of foundation, the date of destruction of the monastery is unknown. It seems most likely that the monastery was abandoned in 1543 when the nearby city of Pécs and the castle of Siklós were taken by the Ottoman army.

---

[1] For a more detailed history of the monastery and discussion on debated sources, see ROMHÁNYI 2000, TAKÁCS 2001, and TAKÁCS 2001 online version on Szent Trinitás: http://paradisum.osb.hu/a51.htm; Recently KISS – SARBAK 2009, 355–356, with further literature.

VII.1: A composite horizontal slice (-100–130 cm) from the ground penetrating radar (GPR) survey of the Holy Trinity monastery superimposed on a satellite image from Google Earth

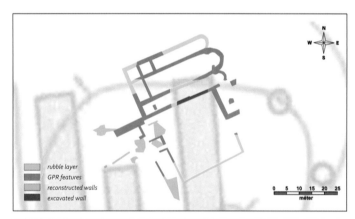

VII.2: Interpretation of the GPR survey

VII.3: Schematic reconstruction in Google Earth of the monastery church and parts of the adjacent buildings based on the ground penetrating radar survey

Archaeological research[2]

During his visit to Vokány in 1957, the historian György Györffy noticed that brick foundation walls, possibly belonging to the monastery, were uncovered during the construction of a silo in the southern part of the village. Lajos Szűcs, the local priest, reported in 1963 that remains of a wall and human bones were found in the same area.

As a result of a rescue excavation led by Olivér Gábor in 2001, several medieval remains and finds were revealed below the floor of a shed belonging to the previously mentioned co-operative farm. The excavators identified an east-west orientated, 1.4 m thick wall section as one of the main walls of the monastery church, but they did not have the opportunity to obtain more information on the plan of the building. The archaeologists found graves on the southern side of the wall and these have been identified as the graves of monks.

Geophysical survey results

In order to put the 2001 excavation results in context, we carried out a geophysical survey on the site in November 2010 and February 2011. We used ground penetrating radar survey instead of magnetometer survey because there were numerous modern ferrous objects and wires in the survey area. In addition, the area had wet soil in both surveys and was made up of various surfaces including gravel, concrete and grass. We carried out the survey using a 0.5 m interval between the scans in a north-south direction.

After processing the data, the survey produced spectacular results in spite of the unfavourable conditions. In the amplitude maps of the first survey in 2010, the walls of a 39 m long typical basilica-type church with a nave, two side aisles, and three apses, immediately became discernible to a depth of 50–70 centimetres. Moreover, the radar anomalies seamlessly correlated with the wall found in 2001. To complete the plan, we organized a second survey in 2011 that showed several details of adjacent buildings including those of the cloister.

Further details of the church were also clarified, such as the foundation walls of the columns that separate the naves, the inner wall of the narthex behind the eastern façade, the foundations of the two bell towers 6.5×6.5 m in size each, and the wall of a room next to the northern belfry. Overgrown by a line of thick bushes, the northeastern portion of the northern aisle and its apse lies below the fence between two properties, and hence it has only a theoretical reconstruction in our survey plan. The nave is 8.5×30.5 m in size, including the apse. The southern aisle is 4 m wide and 19 m long. The apse of the nave extends beyond the apses of the aisles. Neither traces of a crypt nor of a rood screen foundation wall could be detected.

Though uneven in quality and strength at places due to the different state of preservation of the remains, the radar anomalies also indicated the main wall of the church to be 1.4 m thick, similar to the wall section found in 2001.

---

[2] A detailed summary of the archaeological research of the monastery, and the results of the excavation in 2001 can be found in: GÁBOR – SZAJCSÁN 2007, with further literature.

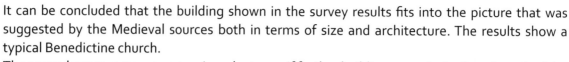

It can be concluded that the building shown in the survey results fits into the picture that was suggested by the Medieval sources both in terms of size and architecture. The results show a typical Benedictine church.

The second survey area was set up in order to see if further buildings were to be found south of the church that may have been parts of the monastery.

It was not possible to survey a large section of these buildings because of the previously mentioned shed that covers them. However, buildings surrounding the cloister became partially visible, and thus the size of the cloister could be determined to be 25×25 m. Possibly the remains of a chapter house, part of a building of significant wall thickness was detected adjoining the south-eastern corner of the church. Traces of another building could be discerned southwest of the church.

Conclusion

As described in several Medieval sources, the location and partial plan of the Benedictine Abbey of Vokány–Trinitáspuszta can be confirmed with certainty with the help of the ground penetrating radar survey. The survey results allow for further conclusions to be drawn; the plan of the Holy Trinity monastery has several close parallels among the contemporary 11–12th century Benedictine monasteries in Hungary. The closest parallels, both in terms of location and plan, are the monasteries at e. g.: Somogyvár, Nagykapornak, and Garamszentbenedek[3] located in Southern and Western Transdanubia, respectively.

---

3   On the so-called "Benedictine type of church" see the critical discussion in SZAKÁCS 2004 with further analogies and literature.

Literature

GÁBOR – SZAJCSÁN 2007
GÁBOR, O. – SZAJCSÁN, É.: A Vokány-Trinitáspuszta lelőhelyen végzett régészeti leletmentés eredményei. In: *Pécsi Arcképek 1 (dr. Bezerédy Győző)*. Pécs 2007, 67–83.

KISS – SARBAK 2009
KISS, G. – SARBAK, G.: Szerzetesi intézmények. In: Fedeles, T. – Sarbak, G. – Sümegi, J.: (szerk.): *A pécsi egyházmegye története I*. Pécs 2009, 337–417.

ROMHÁNYI 2000
ROMHÁNYI, B. F.: *Kolostorok és társaskáptalanok a középkori Magyarországon*. Budapest 2000.

SZAKÁCS 2004
SZAKÁCS, B. Zs.: Állandó alaprajzok – változó vélemények? Megjegyzések a „bencés templomtípus" magyarországi pályafutásához. In: Bodnár, Sz. – Jávor, A. – Lővei, P. – Pataki, G. – Sümegi, Gy. – Szilágyi, A. (eds): *Maradandóság és változás. Művészettörténeti konferencia, Ráckeve, 2000*. Budapest 2004, 25–37.

TAKÁCS 2001
TAKÁCS, I. (ed.): *Paradisum plantavit (Bencés monostorok a középkori Magyarországon)/Benedictine monasteries in Medieval Hungary*. Pannonhalma 2001. The online edition can be accessed at http://paradisum.osb.hu/

VIII. 1526: Mohács … or Majs?
Investigations at the Mohács Battlefield

The site of the first Battle of Mohács in 1526 has the longest history of research among the battlefields in Hungary. Despite this, there are a number of questions still unanswered in connection with the events of the battle. Written by both Christian and Ottoman authors, there are several contemporary and near-contemporary sources that describe or refer to the battle. However, the analysis of these sources by numerous researchers during the last two centuries only produced ambiguous theories on how the troops were deployed and where the decisive events of the battle took place. [1]

Nowadays, the analysis of literary sources can be augmented by archaeological finds and observations, of which even the negative ones can be helpful. Recent archaeological investigations, however, have been hindered by the fact that during the 16th and 17th centuries, several armies, both Christian and Ottoman, camped in the area. These armies left behind objects that, combined with those of the 1526 battle, make the interpretation of the finds difficult. [2]

Attempts to examine the battlefield using classical archaeological methods such as excavation have mainly produced negative results. The only significant result of these investigations was the discovery and excavation of five mass graves by László Papp and Borbála Maráz (Janus Pannonius Museum) during the 1960s and 1970s. The victims buried in these mass graves were Christian prisoners of war beheaded after the battle. [3]

A significant step forward in the research of the battle was the discovery of the site of Földvár, a village mentioned in one of the most important sources that describes the events. Enthusiasts of local history, Béla Kiss[4] and József Szűcs published their findings in a booklet that remained neglected by professional research until 1993, when Lajos Négyesi (Institute and Museum of Military History) first examined the site using methods of battlefield archaeology. [5]

A joint group of researchers from the Janus Pannonius Museum and the Institute and Museum of Military History began a research project at the 1526 Mohács Battlefield. The project has since been supported by the National Cultural Fund of Hungary, the local government of the village of Majs and recently by the ArchaeoLandscapes Europe Project. The participants received help from volunteer students of archaeology and history at the Eötvös Loránd University and Pázmány Péter Catholic University. [6]

The research group chose the suspected site of the late medieval Földvár village as a starting point. There were two reasons for this choice. Firstly, the fact that this village has the most

---

[1] For a comprehensive summary of the latest results of research and the literary sources about the battle see: RÚZSÁS – SZAKÁLY 1986, and recently B. SZABÓ 2006.

[2] NÉGYESI 1994.

[3] PAPP 1960, 1987; MARÁZ 1987; NÉGYESI 2010, 67–68. Recently summarized in B. SZABÓ 2006, 239–264.

[4] KISS 1978.

[5] NÉGYESI 1994.

[6] A more detailed summary of research history and the archaeological results can be found in: BERTÓK – POLGÁR 2011.

VIII.1: Archive vertical aerial photographs showing the location of the suspected late medieval village of Földvár (HM-HIM Archive inv. no. (a) 1953/50408; (b) 1977/3245-78; (c) 1978/5887-79)

detailed description in the sources that can help to identify the battle site. Secondly, some of the decisive events of the battle (such as the initially successful charge, and defeat of the Hungarian heavy cavalry) are likely to have happened in its vicinity.

The research group's general aim has been to complement the information gained from archive literary sources and battlefield archaeological methods with data collected in the field.

These methods include using non-destructive prospection techniques such as aerial reconnaissance, systematic field-walking and geophysical survey in order to shed light on the sequence of events.

It is worth quoting the report by one of the eyewitnesses, István Brodarics, Royal Chancellor[7]:

"The place where the army formed its battle order lay a mile [ca. 8–9 km] from Mohács, and half a mile [ca. 4–4.5 km] from the Danube. Here, as we referred to it previously – there was a wide meadow uninterrupted by scrub, hills or watercourses. There was, however, a muddy wetland overgrown with reed to the left, between us and the Danube. This marsh was one of the places where many died later on.

In front of us lay a long line of hills, like the auditorium of a theatre, beyond which the Turkish Emperor set up his camp. Called Földvár, a small village with a church sloping down from the hill, where the enemy artillery took up its position. Later, towards the end of the battle, we could see with our own eyes that this place was infested by the enemy, among them mainly by the so-called janissaries. They occupied the whole area behind the houses of the village. It became known later that the Emperor was amongst them."

---

7   The English translation by G. Bertók was based on the Hungarian text in BRODARICS 1527. Note that the Hungarian mile of the period was ca. 8.3 km.

VIII.2: Aerial photographs (B. G. 11.04.2011) showing the suspected Földvár village site. The whitish-grey strip of the settlement, as well as the darker strip of its main street is clearly visible in the pictures. Traces of our systematic field-walking show up in Fig VIII.2.c, enlarged from Fig. VII.2.b.

Unlike in the archive images available to us, the portion of the settlement lying west of the north-south running canal clearly shows up in these images. In accordance with the description by I. Brodarics ("a small village with a church sloping down from the hill "), the settlement at this point meets the hills that border the battlefield on the west.

As it was already established by the local historian Béla Kiss, the description by Brodarics can be identified with the settlement site chosen for investigation. From the viewpoint of the Hungarian army, the line of hills located to the east of the present-day village of Majs indeed forms, a background resembling an auditorium and the suspected village of Földvár lies in front of them. The flat area behind the village is large enough to accomodate a larger military unit. Finally, the finds (bullets and other projectiles, fragmented weapons, eastern style horseshoes, etc.) recovered from the area of the suspected village of Földvár indicate that fighting took place in the village.

The main aims of the geophysical survey were to determine the size and extents of the suspected Földvár village, to find possible traces of the Ottoman artillery (according to the report by a surviving German mercenary, Turkish cannons were dug in)[8] and to identify mass graves. The presence of mass graves in the vicinity of the village can be deduced from the following: there are reports indicating that heavy fighting took place in and around Földvár leaving numerous corpses of victims in the area; contemporary literary sources relate that serfs hired by the countess Dorottya Kanizsai buried the dead on the battlefield after the Ottomans left. It seems plausible that they did not carry the decaying corpses a great distance and therefore it is logical to assume that there are several mass graves in the vicinity of Földvár.

Through the application of a set of non-invasive archaeological methods, our goals have at present been partially achieved. Aerial photography, geophysical survey and systematic field-walking helped determine the extents and plan of the eastern half of the village of Földvár. This is true even if the interpretation of the geophysical survey results is sometimes ambiguous due to the fact that they not only show the relevant late medieval, but also some prehistoric, Roman and early medieval features. That the area was occupied in these latter eras is attested to by finds recovered during the systematic field-walking surveys. Among others, such features could be the trenches that cross the village diagonally and features resembling sunken-floor houses that were found in the middle of the main street of the village. It was still possible to delineate the borders of the village, as well as its main street and dwelling houses. Several anomalies are likely to indicate ditches, barns, stables and other structures of a similar nature.

The majority of the finds recovered during the intensive field-walking date to the late medieval period and therefore belong to the settlement that was destroyed in the 1526 battle. The distribution of these finds seems to correspond with the magnetic anomalies aligned to the main street, where the preliminary interpretation indicates late medieval houses. Our metal detector survey produced several coins, projectiles, fragments of weapons, belt buckles, spurs, horseshoes and metal harness-fittings, and a 16th century clasp whose parallels were found in the mass graves excavated a few kilometres away. These finds are most likely to be related to the battle.

Consequently, the first aim of the research plan has been completed successfully, except for locating the church mentioned by I. Brodarics.

We hope that we will have the opportunity to do further to work on the project in order to clarify the ambiguities around this historic event that decided the fate of the Medieval Kingdom of Hungary.

---

[8]   NÉMET ÚJSÁGLAP 1526.

Literature

BERTÓK – POLGÁR 2011
BERTÓK, G. – POLGÁR, B.: A mohácsi csatatér és a középkori Földvár falu régészeti kutatása. *Hadtörténelmi Közlemények* 2011/3, 919–928.

BRODARICS 1527
BRODARICS, I.: Igaz történet a magyarok és Szülejmán török császár mohácsi ütközetéről, 1527. translated by P. Kulcsár. In: SZABÓ, J. B. (ed.): *Mohács. Nemzet és emlékezet.* Budapest 2006, 134–153.

KISS 1978
KISS, B.: *A mohácsi csata. Legújabb kutatások.* Mohács 1978.

MARÁZ 1987
MARÁZ, B.: Újabb tömegsírok a mohácsi csatatéren. In: Katona, T. (ed.): *Mohács emlékezete* (harmadik bővített kiadás). Budapest 1987, 274–279.

NÉGYESI 1994
NÉGYESI, L.: A mohácsi csata. *Hadtörténelmi Közlemények* 1994/4, 62–79.

NÉGYESI 2010
NÉGYESI, L.: *Csaták néma tanúi. A csata- és hadszíntérkutatás– hadtörténeti régészet fogalma és módszerei.* HM Hadtörténeti Intézet és Múzeum, Budapest 2010.

NÉMET ÚJSÁGLAP 1526
NÉMET ÚJSÁGLAP (translated by T. Katona). In: SZABÓ, J. B. (ed.): *Mohács. Nemzet és emlékezet.* Budapest 2006, 131–133.

B. SZABÓ 2006
SZABÓ, J. B. (ed.): *Mohács. Nemzet és emlékezet.* Budapest 2006.

PAPP 1960
PAPP, L.: A mohácsi csatahely kutatása. *JPMÉ* 5 (1960) 237–251.

PAPP 1987
PAPP, L.: A mohácsi csatahely kutatása. In: Katona, T. (ed.): *Mohács emlékezete* (harmadik bővített kiadás). Budapest 1987, 251–271.

RÚZSÁS – SZAKÁLY 1986
RÚZSÁS, L. – SZAKÁLY, F. (ed.): Mohács. *Tanulmányok a mohácsi csata 450. évfordulója alkalmából.* Budapest 1986.

VIII.4: Musket ball mould and lead musket balls
(photos: Lajos Négyesi)

VIII.3 a, b, c: Excavation of the mass graves associated
with the executions following the 1526 Battle of Mohács
near the village of Sátorhely (JPM Archive)

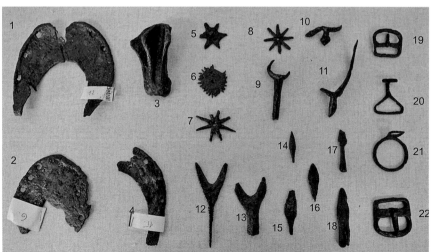

VIII.5: Surface finds, many
of which are of military nature,
from the suspected village of
Földvár and its surroundings:
1–2, 4: horseshoes;
3: mace;
5–11: earlier medieval prick-
and later medieval rowel
spurs;
12–13: arrowheads for hunting
birds;
14–18: military arrowheads/
crossbow bolts;
19–22: belt buckles and fittings

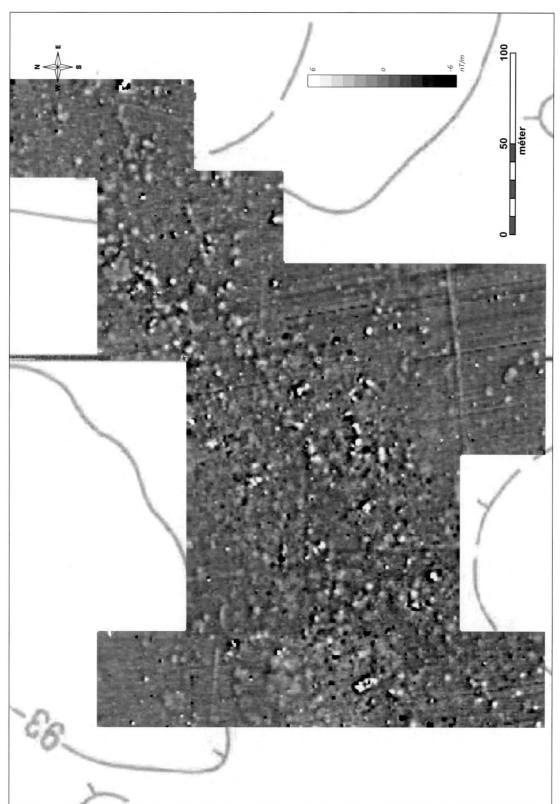

VIII.6: The magnetogram overlaid on the topographic map

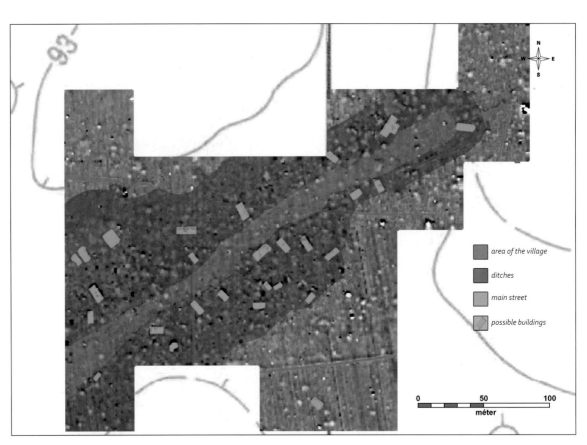

VIII.7: The interpreted magnetogram overlaid on the topographic map

VIII.8: Distribution of Prehistoric finds based on systematic field-walking of two areas of the village (10×10 m grid)

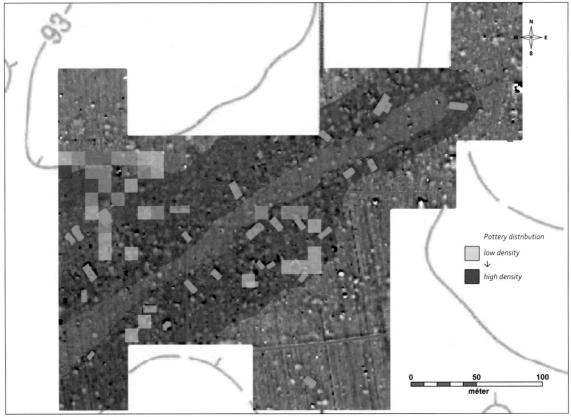

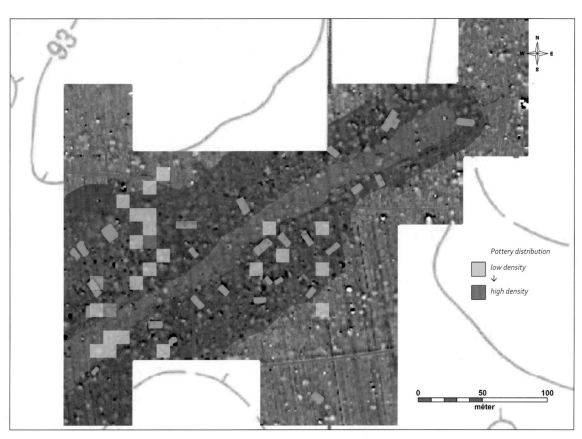

VIII.9: *Distribution of Roman finds based on systematic field-walking of two areas of the village (10×10 m grid)*

VIII.10: *Distribution of late medieval finds based on systematic field-walking of two areas of the village (10×10 m grid)*

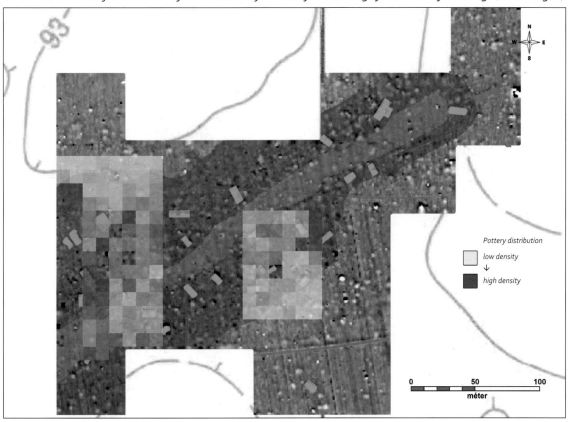

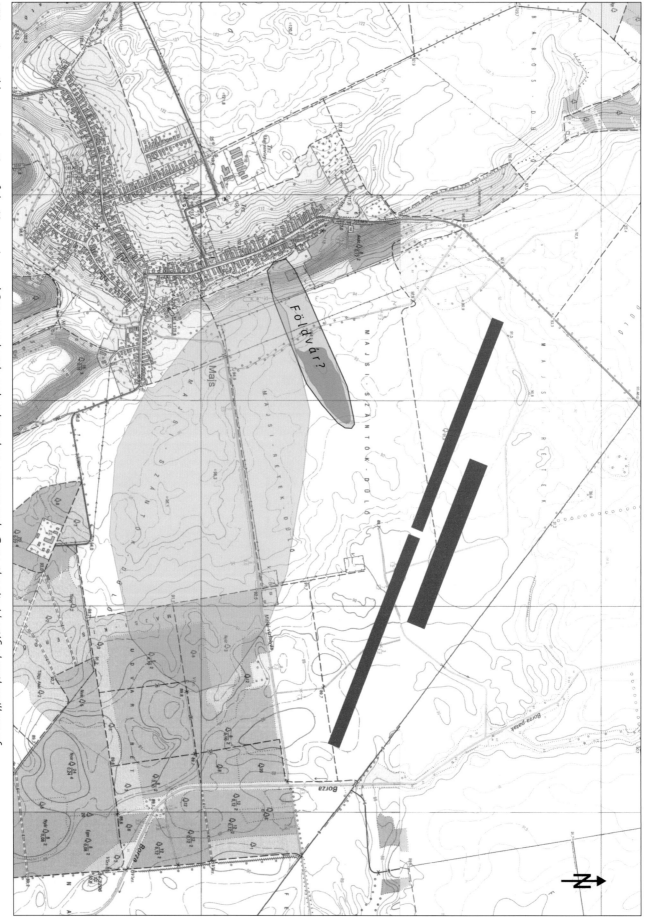

VIII.11: A possible reconstruction of the Hungarian and Ottoman battle orders based on our research. Grey: the site identified as the village of Földvár (the surveyed area is marked with darker grey); red: battle order of the Hungarian army; green: the area occupied by the Rumelian and Anatolian divisions of the Ottoman army before the battle.

Földvár?

Majs

M A J S I   S Z Á N T Ó K · D Ű L Ő

Borza

0   500

Abbreviations

AAH	Acta Archaeologica Academiae Scientiarum Hungaricae, Budapest
ArchHung	Archaeologia Hungarica, Budapest
AÉ	Archaeologiai Értesítő, Budapest
BÁMÉ	Béri Balog Ádám Múzeum Évkönyve, Szekszárd
BRGK	Bericht der Römisch-Germanischen Komission, Berlin
JPMÉ	Janus Pannonius Múzeum Évkönyve, Pécs
MUAG	Mitteilungen der Österreichischen Arbeitsgemeinschaft für Ur- und Frühgeschichte, Wien
MPK	Mitteilung Prähistoruscher Komission, Wien
SMK	Somogy Megyei Múzeumok Évkönyve, Kaposvár
ŠtZ	Študijné zvesti Archeologického ústavu Nitra